Psycholinguistic learning disabilities: diagnosis and remediation

SAMUEL A. KIRK

WINIFRED D. KIRK

University of Illinois Press
Urbana   Chicago   London

Preface

The purpose of this book is to assist those using the ITPA to interpret test results and to organize remedial programs. It would be simple if diagnosis and remediation of learning disabilities involved just giving a test, obtaining a score, and then using a specific remedial approach or particular prepared materials. Unfortunately, diagnosis and remediation of learning disabilities are highly complex and require considerable knowledge of tests, their meaning and limitations, and the kinds of remedial programs that will ameliorate the disability and aid the child in learning.

The first two chapters discuss the broad area of learning disabilities and explain the development and meaning of the subtests of the ITPA. Since considerable research has been conducted with the ITPA, selected studies are reviewed in Chapter 3. A diagnostic-remedial teacher or a psychologist will find research results that will be of value in diagnosis and in interpretation of subtest scores and patterns of disabilities. Those subtests of the ITPA which are correlated with reading disabilities and those which are not have been shown in a number of studies. Those particular deficits or assets which are found in different ethnic groups, the mentally retarded, the cerebral palsied, and other groups have also been studied.

Chapters 4, 5, and 6 deal primarily with the diagnostic process, both in general and specifically with how scores on the ITPA are analyzed and interpreted. Sample patterns of disabilities are described and the procedures by which these patterns are developed are explained in detail.

The ITPA, although consisting of twelve subtests, is not a complete battery for the diagnosis of all learning disabilities. To alert the diagnostician to broader aspects of behavior, Chapter 7, "Suggestions for Further Analysis and Diagnosis," is included. This chapter suggests other tests but also includes teacher observations that correspond to the twelve subtests. A complete diagnosis must therefore include observations of behavior as well as test results. This chapter has also been included to assist the diagnostician and remedial teacher in understanding the levels, processes, and channels that were employed in constructing the test, and in giving ideas for remediation.

The last two chapters provide some guidelines for remediation and include general principles (Chapter 8) and outlines for developing remedial procedures (Chapter 9). These are not remedial methods for each deficit but, rather, general guidelines upon which a remedial teacher can devise a remedial procedure and select the appropriate materials. It is a guide for the remedial teacher rather than a set of lesson plans.

This project was assisted in part by a grant from the Easter Seal Research Foundation of the National Easter Seal Society for Crippled Children and Adults.

Contents

List
of
figures

Figure

Psycholinguistic
learning
disabilities

Chapter one

The
concept
of
learning
disabilities

Traditional school programs for handicapped children tend to identify and classify children according to each one's major handicap. The classification resulting from an assessment of the child leads to placement in one of the existing classes for mentally retarded, deaf, blind, crippled, speech-defective, emotionally disturbed, or subcategories of these such as partially seeing or partially deaf.

Educational authorities have recognized for some time that handicapped children do not always fit into neat, well-defined categories with uniform characteristics. They have recognized that mentally retarded children, even with a narrow IQ range, are not homogeneous in characteristics, and that not all deaf children learn at the same rate. One deaf child might learn speech reading while another unfortunately does not. One child may be classified as cerebral palsied but may also be mentally retarded, while another cerebral-palsied child may learn adequately in school or may even become a college student.

To make matters worse there are a number of children who are not deaf, not blind, not mentally retarded, but who are unable to learn under ordinary school instruction. This is the group that has come under the heading of "specific learning disabilities."

What are specific learning disabilities?

The concept of learning disabilities has recently evolved to encompass the heterogeneous group of children not fitting neatly into the traditional categories of handicapped children. There is a substantial number of children who show retardation in learning to talk, who do not develop language facility, who do not develop normal visual or auditory perception, or who have great difficulty in learning to read, spell, write, or make arithmetic calculations. Some of them are not receptive to language but are not deaf, some are not able to perceive visually but are not blind, and some cannot learn by ordinary methods of instruction but are not mentally retarded. Although these children form a heterogeneous group and fail to learn for diverse reasons, they have one thing in common: developmental discrepancies in abilities. The term "learning disability" has been defined in different ways depending upon the emphasis of the author. The National Advisory Committee for the Handicapped studied this problem and formulated the following widely accepted definition:

> *Children with special (specific) learning disabilities exhibit a disorder in one or more of the basic psychological processes involved in understanding or in using spoken or written language. These may be manifested in disorders of listening, thinking, talking, reading, writing, spelling, or arithmetic. They include conditions which have been referred to as perceptual handicaps, brain injury, minimal brain dysfunction, dyslexia, developmental aphasia, etc. They do not include learning problems which are due primarily to visual, hearing, or motor handicaps, to mental retardation, emotional disturbance, or to environmental disadvantage.* *

The word "special," or "specific," is very important in this definition since it indicates that the child has a definite retardation in one or more areas but that this retardation is not caused by a sensory deficit or severe mental retardation, and that it exists in spite of the fact that the child has certain abilities in other areas. It also indicates that the child's retardation is not due to lack of educational experiences.

It should be emphasized, however, that not all children who

---

* "Notes and Working Papers . . . ," *Education of Handicapped Children.* Prepared for the Subcommittee on Education of the Committee on Labor and Public Welfare, United States Congress (Washington, D.C.: U.S. Government Printing Office, May, 1968), p. 14.

show retardation in school can be considered children with learning disabilities. A deaf child, for example, has a language disability and a speech disability; yet he cannot be classified as having a learning disability since his retardation in language and speech is the result of his inability to hear. A severely mentally defective child may show extreme retardation in language, speech, and all other communication processes. This child does not necessarily have a learning disability since the term "learning disability" implies certain assets in addition to specific disabilities or wide discrepancy between abilities. At the same time some children who appear mentally retarded in the classroom and on intelligence tests may be children with learning disabilities rather than children who are mentally retarded.

The failure to differentiate clearly between specific learning disabilities and other types of handicaps has caused great confusion. Some of the case studies presented later will exemplify this point.

It should also be noted that there is often an overlap of handicapping conditions in the same child, with learning disabilities and other handicapping conditions both being present. Included in this set of children with learning disabilities are those who have also been classified as crippled, emotionally disturbed, and so forth. Some children are difficult to classify because (a) they have both a learning disability and another identifiable exceptionality (e.g., gifted but with a learning disability or emotionally disturbed plus a learning disability); or (b) they have a learning disability which sometimes misclassifies them as having a traditional form of exceptionality (e.g., a child who is misclassified as mentally retarded because of a low score on intelligence tests but who, upon more intensive assessment, is found to have normal abilities in some areas and very deficient abilities in other areas). These latter children will benefit most if their learning disability is treated directly while classroom adjustment is provided for their other types of handicaps. It is not sufficient merely to place them in a special class for the other handicap and assume that the learning disability will take care of itself.

It has been found, for example, that some children assigned to classes for the emotionally disturbed have severe conduct disorders and at the same time have a severe learning disability, such as an inability to learn to read or receptive or expressive language disorders. In these cases the child must be remediated for both handicaps. In other cases of children assigned to classes for the emotionally disturbed it has been found that the learning disability is primary and that its amelioration through remediation improves the conduct disorder and permits the child to function normally in the regular classroom. Similarly, some children who are classified as mentally retarded and placed in special classes need further diagnosis to determine if they are average or superior in some psychological functions and very deficient in others. Such children tend to score low in IQ, since the score depends on a composite of abilities which may classify them as mentally retarded. Some of these children, after remediation of their specific deficits, have qualified for regular classes instead of classes for the mentally retarded.

Terminology

Children with specific learning problems who are not classified under the traditional categories of deafness, blindness, crippling conditions, emotional disturbance, mental retardation, etc. sometimes defy classification partly because of confusion in terminology. There have arisen in the literature numerous labels for aberrations in behavior, development, and learning. In general, the terms used to describe these aberrations fall into two broad categories, (a) etiological and (b) behavioral.

Etiological terms. Medical terminology tends to label learning disorders in terms of etiology and generally relates them to deficits in the brain. Terms such as brain injury, brain damage, minimal cerebral dysfunction, neurophysiological dysynchrony, organic disorder, central nervous system disorder, psychoneurological disorder, etc. are terms which imply a neurological etiology as an explanation for the deviation in development.

Behavioral terms. Behavioral terms attempt to label the disordered function according to behavioral manifestations. These behavioral terms include: perceptual handicap, conceptual disorders, reading disability (dyslexia), catastrophic behavior, developmental imbalance, learning disability, and various subcategories of the term "aphasia." Aphasia was originally used to denote the loss of different aspects of language ability after they had been acquired. Work in the field of aphasia has been conducted primarily with adults in whom the acquired ability has been lost as a result of disease or accident affecting the brain. The term is not strictly usable for children who have developmental disorders, i.e., have not yet acquired language. They have not lost anything—

they have failed to acquire something. It is therefore preferable to use other terms with these children, terms that do not necessarily imply a brain deficit or brain damage, even though this can be inferred in many instances.

The term "learning disability" does not include all aberrations of development. It is more specific to educational development and is concerned primarily with disorders of the communication process. The term "learning disability" is, then, primarily an educational concept. Its focus is on behavioral diagnosis and remediation rather than on biological etiology and the discovery of correlated central nervous system deficits. Children with learning disorders in the perceptual, conceptual, language, or academic subject areas tend in many instances to have correlated behavior disorders of hyperactivity, lack of attention, and general maladaptive behavior. But not all children who exhibit behavior disorders could be classified as children with learning disabilities requiring special remediation.

The material which follows describes some of the more common forms of learning disorders which require special remediation and which constitute the essential categories under the general caption of learning disabilities.

Types of learning disabilities

Any attempt to categorize disorders in children runs the risk of ignoring the overlap with another category and/or the compounding of disorders with one another. For the purpose of clarity, however, the following types of learning disorders have been grouped under three rubrics: (a) academic disorders, (b) nonsymbolic disorders, and (c) symbolic disorders. In so doing it should be recognized that one disorder may be basic to another. An academic disability such as reading disability may relate to nonsymbolic disorder of perception, which is the psychological deficit that can inhibit the child's ability to learn to read. This perceptual disorder can sometimes be traced to a neurological handicap, but for remedial purposes the academic disability and the psychological deficit become the essential factors in the diagnosis which make it possible to organize remedial instruction.

Academic disabilities

There are many forms of academic disabilities but only the most common ones of reading, writing, and arithmetic will be discussed here.

Reading disability. This condition is not uncommon in school children but is also confused with other forms of reading failure. Some children, because of environmental or instructional factors, are retarded in reading but show nothing abnormal within themselves. Such retardation is most often amenable to corrective reading, since the child is developing normally in psychological abilities but requires developmental and correctional forms of instruction in a classroom. The child with a true reading disability is one who is diagnosed as having a deficit in the development of psychological characteristics basic to the acquisition of academic skills. A vast number of labels have been used to describe such conditions, including such terms as word blindness, strephosymbolia, congenital alexia, dyslexia, congenital symbolamblyopia, bradylexia, specific reading disability, amnesia visualis, and other terms. In describing children with such deficits, Marion Monroe (1932) used a behavioral or educational term as the title of her book, *Children Who Cannot Read.* The present writers prefer the latter term with the addition, "because of psychological developmental deficits."

Writing disabilities. Some children have difficulty in learning to write due to some deficit related to motor encoding or other psychological function. In the medical literature this condition is sometimes referred to as agraphia or dysgraphia.

Arithmetic disabilities. Some children have difficulty in acquiring quantitative concepts due to some possible psychological deficits, such as defective auditory memory, auditory association, space orientation, and so forth. In the medical literature arithmetic disabilities are referred to as acalculia or dyscalculia.

Nonsymbolic disabilities

The term "nonsymbolic disabilities" refers to the inability to recognize, integrate, or use sense impressions. The disorders described below are illustrative of this type of developmental deficit. Some of these are explained in the following paragraphs.

Perceptual disabilities. Children with perceptual disorders are those whose sensory abilities are intact but who do not perceive, discriminate, or recognize efficiently in one or more sense modalities. A child who can hear sounds but is unable to discriminate or recognize them is said to have an auditory perceptual problem. A child who cannot recognize the faces of his classmates until he hears their voices is one who has a visual perceptual disorder. A child who is unable to localize the finger that is touched but knows that one of the fingers has been touched is one who has a tactual perceptual disability. In the medical literature these children are sometimes considered to have auditory agnosia, visual agnosia, or tactual agnosia. In addition there are disturbances in speed of perception, figure-ground discrimination, closure ability, or other difficulties dealing primarily with auditory and visual nonsymbolic perceptual problems.

Expressive nonsymbolic disabilities. Children who have an inability in imitating vocally or manually or who have not acquired a repertoire of manual or vocal expressive habits are sometimes diagnosed in medicine as apraxic. In this condition the child may perceive a command but be unable to carry out the act, or he may have a faulty conception of a movement, or be confused in carrying out a complicated act, or be unable to manipulate objects even though the motor functions are intact. Disabilities in writing or in speaking may have their origin in this nonsymbolic expressive dysfunction.

Linguistic or symbolic disabilities

When a child can hear but cannot understand the meaning of the spoken word or is delayed or retarded in understanding the spoken word, he may be said to have an auditory receptive (symbolic or representational) disability. This is sometimes called sensory or receptive aphasia. Likewise, when the child is unable to attach meaning to what he sees or to what has been presented to him visually, he may be said to have a visual receptive disorder.

When a child has difficulty in expressing ideas vocally or manually, the child may be said to have a symbolic or representational expressive disability. This disability has been referred to in adults as expressive or motor aphasia.

Testing individual differences

Since the beginning of the century, especially after the invention of the Binet-Simon intelligence scales, psychologists have been actively engaged in the development of measuring instruments to assess intelligence, achievement, interests, attitudes, and personality. The purpose of many of these tests has been primarily to classify individuals for placement purposes.

Clinicians and special educators find that classification and placement of children in nominal categories is of limited value. In dealing with deviant children, the primary concern is, through formal or informal methods of evaluation, to delineate abilities and disabilities and to organize instructional materials to ameliorate deficits in psychological abilities and academic achievement. These demands have led to a reconsideration of the purposes of psychometric instruments and a reassessment of (a) the concepts of classification and diagnosis and (b) the concept of individual differences.

Classification and diagnostic tests

Most of our current psychometric and achievement tests have been used primarily for classification purposes. They generally yield a total score to allow classification into broad categories for placement purposes. Tests that yield only an MA or an IQ or tests that yield only a grade score may be considered classification tests. A typical reading achievement test, for example, renders a reading grade or a reading age. A child of nine years of age with an IQ of 105 who is currently in the fifth grade may achieve a reading score of grade 2.5. These scores classify this child as an intellectually average fifth-grade child but who is reading at the second-grade level. The scores show a marked discrepancy between his mental ability and his reading achievement, thus classifying the child as a reading disability case. This information is, of course, valuable but actually does not pinpoint the areas of difficulty the child has so that the teacher can institute proper remedial training.

In addition to knowing a child's intellectual ability and his achievement level, a teacher is interested primarily in the kinds of information which will assist her in organizing a remedial program to correct the reading disability. This type of information is obtained from a diagnostic reading test. A diagnostic reading test differs from a general reading test in that the former analyzes the process by which the child attempts to read. An analysis of such specific errors and faulty habits as vowel errors, consonant errors, substitutions, slow reading, repetitions in reading, methods of word attack, etc. is usually provided by a diagnostic reading test. Following this type of analysis or diagnosis, the teacher is in a better position to design instructional methods and materials to correct the child's basic errors in reading and hence to remove or remediate the reading disability. It is for this reason that diagnostic tests have been organized and have been used in relation to remedial instruction.

A diagnostic test, therefore, is a test that assesses specific abilities, disabilities, and achievements of a child in such a way that remediation of defects can logically follow. Diagnostic tests attempt to identify specifically the various disabilities or faulty habits used in the acquisition of academic skills of reading, writing, spelling, and arithmetic and in the various psychological functions involved in the processes of thinking, listening, talking, and perceiving. An example in the intellectual field is found in Leon Thurstone's (1938) analysis of intelligence into primary mental abilities and in Thelma G. Thurstone's (1949) early program of remediation of primary mental abilities through instructional materials.

The dissatisfaction with classification instruments has led to the recent development of tests for specific functions that give clues to remediation. The Illinois Test of Psycholinguistic Abilities (ITPA), among others, represents an effort along these lines.

Inter- and intraindividual differences

The term "individual differences" can have dual meaning. The most common usage of the term in a classroom refers to interindividual differences, namely, variability among members of a group. A test that yields an MA or an IQ or a reading score may be considered a classification test since it views individual differences in this sense. In this way children can be placed in groups according to their ability, thus making possible variation of instruction in order to reach both the bright and the dull, those with normal hearing or vision and those with defective hearing or vision, and those with other variations in abilities. The concept of interindividual differences led to the development of testing programs to determine relative abilities of children in a classroom. It also led to broader categories whereby children were classified for placement in special classes. This has been found administratively helpful but educationally unproductive. The statement that a child has a low IQ or is at the 25th percentile in his reading class does not necessarily lead to educationally relevant hypotheses for remediation.

Although the term "individual differences" usually conjures up the concept of differences among children, there is a different concept which is more meaningful in the area of remediation. This concept places the emphasis not on interindividual differences but on intraindividual differences, which are the basis upon which differentiation of exceptional children and programs has been made (Kirk, 1962). "Intraindividual differences" is a less common meaning of the term "individual differences." This concept directs attention not to the comparison of one child with another but to differences of ability within a single child. In other words, the concept of intraindividual differences led logically to psychometric tests that could measure a number of specific and discrete areas of psycho-educational development. These areas could then be compared to determine discrepancies in growth and developmental imbalances within the child himself. Such an assessment is diagnostic rather than classificatory, since it pinpoints underlying areas of deficiency basic to the observable problem. It also delineates abilities that can be utilized as springboards from which to develop the deficient areas. Diagnostic reading tests are tests of intraindividual differences and tend to outline abilities or disabilities in reading within a single child. The Illinois Test of Psycholinguistic Abilities is a comparable diagnostic intraindividual test of psychological and linguistic functions. Its principal use is to diagnose a child's psycho-linguistic abilities so that remediation can follow.

Summary statement

The concept of learning disability demands a relatively new educational approach which involves handicapped children with specific disorders in perceiving, thinking, listening, talking, reading, writing, spelling, arithmetic, and related disabilities primarily in the communication process. Although there may be an overlap among these disabilities and other handicaps, these disorders are discrete as related to the traditional categories of such handicapping conditions as mental retardation, emotional disturbance, crippling conditions, deafness, blindness, and speech defects, all of which are included in special education programs.

The disabilities in children that are now grouped under the category of learning disability have historically had the attention of a number of disciplines, particularly neurologists who were interested in the relation of brain dysfunction in adults and the consequent loss of the ability to speak (aphasia), to write (agraphia), or to read (alexia). Studies on adults with brain damage have led many to believe that children who have difficulty in acquiring language, speech, or reading skills must have a developmental deficit within the brain which accounts for the difficulty in learning: hence the historical emphasis on terminology that describes brain dysfunction as etiological.

The concept of learning disability as used in education does not deny or reject a neurological deficit (acquired, genetic, or otherwise) but neither does it depend on a neurological determination.

The major emphasis is on the use of psychological tests and/or observation for the purpose of organizing a remedial educational program. Such a program is rarely dependent upon a neurological or biological diagnosis but is very dependent upon the determination of psychological abilities and disabilities. This concept has led to the use of the term "specific learning disability" instead of "brain damage" in psychoeducational circles, since the task is psychoeducational diagnosis and educational remediation. The concept of learning disability is an extension of the concept of intraindividual differences (discrepancies in growth within a single child) as contrasted to the more common concept of interindividual differences (differences between children in a class). The concept of intraindividual differences has necessitated the development of diagnostic psychoeducational tests.

Chapter two

The development of the ITPA

While the medical specialist is concerned primarily with etiology and with the relationship between communication disorders and a possible cerebral dysfunction in children, the special educator is concerned primarily with the assessment of the behavioral symptoms and with special methods of ameliorating the disability. In education a child who has the basic potential to learn, but does not learn after adequate instruction, is probably a child with a learning disability. The knowledge of the etiology of the disability in most instances is not helpful to the organization of remedial procedures. Labeling a child as brain-injured (usually inferred from behavior) does not, with the exception of rare instances, alter the remedial procedure.

Early attempts at diagnosis

With school-age children the diagnosis of learning disability is generally preceded by failure in academic subjects. In preschool children the disabilities are primarily in behavior and the communication processes. Such problems with young children presented themselves to us and our associates when we were conducting an experiment in the early education of the mentally retarded as far back as 1949. During this period it was apparent that many young children needed evaluation and diagnosis so that a specific educational program could be provided. Among the group were a number of children who were classified as mentally retarded but who had such specific disabilities as language, perceptual, and behavior disorders.

Like that of many clinicians, the diagnosis used was informal since few adequate tests (apart from general intelligence tests) were available for the evaluation of the language and perceptual abilities of these children. Adopting customary clinical procedure, data from such tests as the Stanford-Binet, the Kuhlmann Tests of Mental Development, and the Vineland Social Maturity Scale were analyzed. Observations were also made of the children's behavior and their responses to intellectual tasks. The diagnostic tools were clearly inadequate.

One five-year-old girl, for instance, had been diagnosed not only as mentally retarded (IQ 50 to 60) but also as legally blind following rubella. She had marked nystagmus but could see and recognize some pictures if given sufficient time. She showed some ability to recognize pictures in spite of her nystagmus and the diagnosis by the ophthalmologist as "legally blind." In addition to the regular preschool program of the experiment, an effort was made to develop her speed of perception and increase her recognition of visual objects by specific exercises devised to make use of the very limited fixations allowed by her nystagmus. A program was designed to train her to respond to pictures utilizing a tachistoscope, beginning initially with an exposure as long as was needed and decreasing to an exposure of 1/25 of a second. This training on an individualized basis for half an hour a day continued for six months. At the conclusion of this training the girl was not only labeling pictures after an exposure of 1/25 of a second but was also interpreting many details of a complex picture and was able to talk about the picture meaningfully. It was felt by the teachers that she was no longer legally blind. A second diagnosis by the ophthalmologist, however, indicated no change on tests of vision. The ophthalmologist was surprised at the improvement in her ability to interpret complex pictures and attributed her improved visual recognition abilities to the training and improvement in central perceptual processes rather than to any change in her nystagmus or visual acuity. This training, combined with the general preschool training, produced a girl who at the age of nine was borderline in intelligence

(IQ 70 to 80) and was able to read and write at the second-grade level (Kirk, 1958, pp. 26–28).

Another child had been diagnosed as both sensory-aphasic and mentally deficient with a Binet IQ of 37. Special training in the auditory receptive process on an individualized basis, together with preschool experience, resulted in a marked improvement in this child. Her later IQ, tested at the age of nine, was 80 (Kirk, 1958, pp. 31–35). Other cases in the preschool demonstrated quite clearly the need for an analytical diagnostic test which would help to pinpoint specific disabilities in these children and from which special remedial programs could be organized.

The experimental edition of the ITPA

Attempts to develop a comprehensive diagnostic test for pre-school children began in 1951, and by 1961 an experimental edition of the ITPA resulted. The background and theoretical basis have been reported by Sievers (1955), McCarthy (1957), Kirk and McCarthy (1961), McCarthy and Kirk (1961), Kirk (1966), and Kirk (1968).

The experimental edition of the Illinois Test of Psycholinguistic Abilities (1961) attempted to isolate specific skills uncontaminated by other functions. One of the major difficulties encountered was developing tests that could be used with two- and three-year-old children. The customary digit repetition test as administered in the Stanford-Binet and WISC, for example, could not be used success-fully with very young children, nor did it discriminate adequately between children at each chronological age level. In order to over-come these difficulties, several modifications were made. One modi-fication in procedure was to give the child a second chance with each sequence of digits if he failed on the first attempt. The time interval between digits was also reduced. Instead of using one sec-ond between each digit as on the Stanford-Binet, we found that younger children could repeat the digits more readily if we pre-sented them at half-second intervals. By using these two changes in technique, we were able to develop an auditory sequential mem-ory test which discriminated among children at different age levels and measured the ability of younger children.

Another problem was that of having each test assess a discrete psychological function. It was desired, for example, that auditory decoding measure only the understanding of verbal receptive ability, without the requirements of a visual stimulus or a verbal response. The test consequently required a response of only "yes" or "no" or a nod of the head.

At this stage in the development of the ITPA it was decided that, rather than undertake another five years of developmental research in order to refine the tests still further, they should be standardized and published as an experimental edition so that their general usefulness and validity could be more widely evaluated.

The nine subtests of the battery that appeared most relevant were Auditory Decoding, Visual Decoding, Auditory-Vocal Association, Visual-Motor Association, Vocal Encoding, Motor Encoding, Auditory-Vocal Automatic (grammatic closure), Auditory-Vocal Sequencing, and Visual-Motor Sequencing. These tests were standardized on 700 children of ages two to nine. A complete description of the rationale, theory, construction, and standardization of the experimental edition of the ITPA has been reported by McCarthy and Kirk (1963).

The revised edition of the ITPA

After five years of clinical use and the accumulation of many research findings, it was apparent that the ITPA had merit and should be put into final form. The knowledge which had been gained about each of the subtests and the test as a whole suggested certain modifications, but it was believed that the basic design of the test was sound and should be maintained.

Over a three-year period (1965–1968) the test materials and procedures were redesigned and the test restandardized, utilizing wherever possible the effective aspects of the original test. The following goals were utilized in the process of development:

1. Time for the total test presentation was to be less than one hour.

2. Recording and scoring were to be quick, easy, and objective.

3. Each subtest was to measure one and only one discrete function.

4. These functions were to be put in the context of life situations wherever possible.

5. Each item within a subtest was to tap essentially the same aspect or facet of ability.

6. Consideration was to be given to such practical features as high interest value to the child, ease of administration and scoring,

minimal space requirements for storing and presenting test materials, and portability and durability of test materials.

In addition to many minor differences between the experimental and the revised editions (for example, terminology, order of presentation, basals and ceilings, exposure times), the revised edition produced some major changes which include the following:

1. The addition of three entirely new tests: Visual Closure (which tests an important area untapped by the experimental edition), Auditory Closure, and Sound Blending (two supplementary tests).

2. Radical revision of two tests: Grammatic Closure (based on the Auditory-Vocal Automatic subtest of the experimental edition) and Visual Sequential Memory (for which the chips were redesigned to minimize possibilities of vocalization).

3. Sampling procedures have been introduced on two tests (both of the sequential memory tests), making it possible to find more quickly the appropriate level of ability for a particular child, thus shortening the time required for the test.

4. One test (Visual Association) has been extended to include a section of visual analogies comparable to the auditory analogies in the Auditory Association test. This raises the age level to which this test is applicable.

5. Directions have been made more explicit, notably on the Verbal Expression and Visual Sequential Memory tests, on the demonstration items, and in handling unusual responses.

6. An improved Record Form makes recording and scoring easier and more accurate.

7. There are fewer objects to manipulate.

8. The norms have been extended upward to ten years of age.

The revised edition of the Illinois Test of Psycholinguistic Abilities was published in the fall of 1968. Further details regarding the construction and standardization of the revised edition can be found in Paraskevopoulos and Kirk (1969).

The clinical model of the ITPA

The hypothetical construct on which the ITPA is based relates those functions whereby the intentions of one individual are trans-

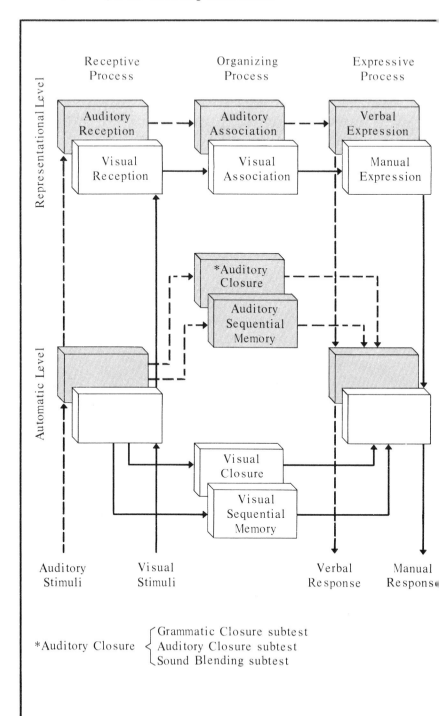

| | Receptive Process | Organizing Process | Expressive Process |

Representational Level

| Auditory Reception | Auditory Association | Verbal Expression |
| Visual Reception | Visual Association | Manual Expression |

Automatic Level

*Auditory Closure

Auditory Sequential Memory

Visual Closure

Visual Sequential Memory

Auditory Stimuli   Visual Stimuli   Verbal Response   Manual Response

*Auditory Closure   { Grammatic Closure subtest   Auditory Closure subtest   Sound Blending subtest

mitted (verbally or nonverbally) to another individual and, reciprocally, functions whereby the environment or the intentions of another individual are received and interpreted. It attempts to interrelate the processes which are involved, for example, when one person receives a message, interprets it, or becomes the source of a new signal to be transmitted. It deals with the psychological functions of the individual which operate in communication activities.

Presenting the theoretical basis for the ITPA can be simplified by offering a graphic representation of the functions which operate during communication activities. The model presented in Figure 2-1 demonstrates graphically the interrelationships of the various functions tested by the ITPA. It will be noted that three dimensions are represented and that at each point where the three dimensions intersect there is indicated a discrete function. These are the separate functions tested by the ITPA. The unlabeled boxes in the model represent areas not tapped by the ITPA and will be explained later.

A description of the three dimensions follows.

Channels of communication

These are the routes through which the content of communication flows. Included here are the modalities through which sense impressions are received and the forms of expression through which a response is made. The channels may include various combinations of sensory input and response output. The major modes of input are auditory and visual; those of output are vocal and motor. Many combinations of input and output are possible, but due to practical limitations, the ITPA incorporates only two:

1. The auditory-vocal channel, i.e., the course by which sensory impressions are received through the ear and responses expressed verbally. This channel is represented in the model by the shaded boxes in the background connected by dotted lines.

2. The visual-motor channel, i.e., the course by which sensory impressions are received through the eye and responses expressed through gesture or movement. In the model this channel is represented by the boxes in the foreground connected by solid lines.

re 2-1
cal model of the ITPA.

Psycholinguistic processes

In analyzing behavior which occurs in the acquisition and use of language, three main processes are considered:

1. The receptive process, i.e., recognition and/or understanding of what is (a) seen or (b) heard. This process is represented in the model by all of the boxes on the left.

2. The organizing process, i.e., eduction of relationships from what is or has been (a) seen or (b) heard. This process is represented in the model by all of the boxes in the center.

3. The expressive process, i.e., the use of those skills necessary to express ideas (a) verbally or (b) by gesture or movement. This process is represented in the model by all the boxes on the right.

Levels of organization of communication habits

The degree to which communication behavior is organized within the individual determines the level of functioning. Two levels are postulated in the clinical model of the ITPA:

1. The representational level includes behavior which requires the more complex mediating process of utilizing symbols which carry the meaning. This level is represented in the model by all of the boxes placed horizontally at the top.

2. The automatic level includes communication behavior requiring less voluntary but highly organized and integrated patterns. This includes such activities as visual and auditory closure, speed of perception, ability to reproduce a sequence seen or heard, rote learning, synthesizing isolated sounds into a word, and utilizing the redundancies of experience. This level is represented in the model by all of the boxes placed horizontally at the bottom.

It will be noted that in the model some boxes have been left blank. These represent areas which are not tapped by the ITPA. There are no tests attempting to measure purely receptive or purely expressive processes at the automatic level. It has been found that isolating the three processes at this level is tenuous and theoretically problematic. Interpretation of test results rests on firmer ground in utilizing "whole level" tests, since it is difficult to free tasks at this level from contamination with other functions. Tests of the receptive process at the automatic level would probably involve tasks of recognition and awareness of stimuli and auditory and visual discrimination abilities. The expressive process at the automatic level involves the ability to perform those routine acts of speech and movement which make communication possible.

It should also be noted that the automatic level has been bifurcated to involve two types of ability. The first is the ability to repeat a sequence of nonmeaningful stimuli, referred to in the model as "sequential memory." The second is the ability to recognize a common unit of experience when only part of it is presented (and/or the somewhat related ability to synthesize isolated parts into a whole). This second ability is referred to in the model as "closure" and involves three tests in the auditory-vocal channel and one in the visual-motor channel.

ITPA subtests

The subtests of the ITPA which were generated from this model tap discrete functions which are incorporated in the three dimensions just discussed. Each utilizes a channel, a level, and a process. It will be noted from the model that the following functions, each of which is tested by a separate subtest of the ITPA, occur at discrete intersections of the three dimensions described above.

1. Auditory Reception (the ability to understand auditory symbols such as verbal discourse) is represented at the intersection of the receptive process, the auditory-vocal channel, and the representational level.

2. Visual Reception (the ability to gain meaning from visual symbols) is represented at the intersection of the receptive process, the visual-motor channel, and the representational level.

3. Auditory Association (the ability to relate concepts presented orally) is represented at the intersection of the organizing process, the auditory-vocal channel, and the representational level.

4. Visual Association (the ability to relate concepts presented visually) is represented at the intersection of the organizing process, the visual-motor channel, and the representational level.

5. Verbal Expression (the ability to express concepts verbally, i.e., vocally) is represented at the intersection of the expressive process, the auditory-vocal channel, and the representational level.

6. Manual Expression (the ability to express ideas manually) is

represented at the intersection of the expressive process, the visual-motor channel, and the representational level.

7. Grammatic Closure (the ability to make use of the redundancies of oral language in acquiring automatic habits for handling syntax and grammatic inflections) is represented at the intersection of the organizing process, the auditory-vocal channel, and the automatic level. The two supplementary tests of Auditory Closure and Sound Blending also fall at this intersection.

8. Visual Closure (the ability to identify a common object from an incomplete visual presentation) is represented at the intersection of the organizing process, the visual-motor channel, and the automatic level.

9. Auditory Sequential Memory (the ability to reproduce from memory sequences of digits of increasing length) is represented at the intersection of the organizing process, the auditory-vocal channel, and the automatic level.

10. Visual Sequential Memory (the ability to reproduce sequences of nonmeaningful figures from memory) is represented at the intersection of the organizing process, the visual-motor channel, and the automatic level.

The twelve tests of the ITPA and some of the everyday behavior which parallel them will be discussed in greater detail in Chapter 7 in relation to supplementary diagnostic programs.

Chapter three

Selected research findings

Much research has developed from the ITPA. In addition to statistical studies on the reliability, validity, and factor loadings of the ITPA subtests, there have been numerous studies on the special abilities and disabilities of different groups of children and studies on the effects of remediation. Bateman has reviewed the research studies using the experimental edition of the ITPA (Bateman, 1965), but like most publications of this nature in an expanding field, the review became outdated almost as soon as it was off the press.

The bulk of the research has, understandably, utilized the experimental edition since at the present writing the revised edition has not been in existence long enough to accumulate a backlog of research. Preliminary findings, however, suggest that parallel research using the two editions point to similar conclusions, as will be indicated in the following pages where a few overlapping studies have been reported. Most of the research reported in this chapter is based on the experimental edition, supplemented wherever possible by reports of research using the revised edition.

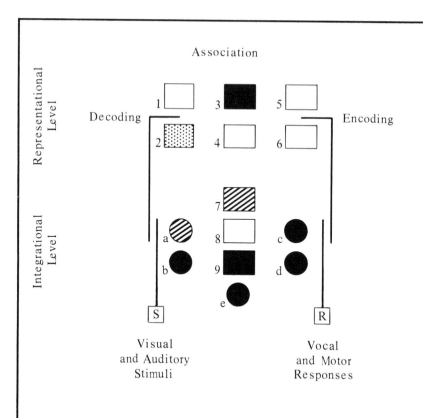

Strength   Marginal deficit

No deficit   Deficit

Representational level
1. Auditory decoding
2. Visual decoding
3. Auditory-vocal association
4. Visual-motor association
5. Vocal encoding
6. Motor encoding

Integrational level
7. Auditory-vocal automatic
8. Auditory-vocal sequential
9. Visual-motor sequential
a. Visual automatic (closure)
b. Sound blending (Monroe)
c. Mazes (WISC)
d. Memory for designs
(Graham-Kendall)
e. Perceptual speed (PMA)

Psycholinguistic characteristics
of special groups of children

Research workers have examined different groups of children to determine their responses to the subtests of the ITPA. The studies that will be summarized here relate to representative investigations relating to (a) severe reading disabilities, (b) speech disorders, (c) mental retardation, (d) mongoloid children, (e) ethnic groups, (f) cerebral-palsied children, and (g) children with visual and auditory handicaps. The results of the studies and their findings will be discussed below.

Severe reading disabilities (dyslexia)

Several studies have been made on the relationship of the ITPA or some of its subtests to reading disabilities. Corrine Kass (1966) found that there is a relationship between difficulty in learning to read and performance on tests at the automatic level, including tests of perceptual speed, closure, and visual memory. The results of Kass's findings are reproduced here to indicate the differences between the automatic (integrational) and the representational (symbolic) levels for children who are retarded in reading during the early grades.

It will be noted from Figure 3-1 that the basic psychological deficiencies among children with reading difficulties are primarily at the automatic level rather than at the representational level. Children with reading problems, according to this study, have greater deficits at the automatic or integrational level as compared to their abilities at the more conceptual, representational (or symbolic) level. It is interesting to note that for the dyslexics the one superior ability was at the representational level. This was the ability to interpret pictures. It is probable that children with severe reading disabilities have relied on this ability to obtain contextual clues from the pictures in books since they were unable to learn to read the words.

Macione (1969) conducted a similar study with twenty-eight

e 3-1

:al model of reading processes indicating areas
ength, no deficit, marginal deficit,
eficit.

e: Kass (1966).

disabled and twenty-eight nondisabled readers in the second and third grades using the revised edition (1968) of the Illinois Test of Psycholinguistic Abilities. Figure 3-2 presents the scaled score profiles of the two groups. It will be noted from the profile that five of the automatic-level tests are lower for the disabled group. Four

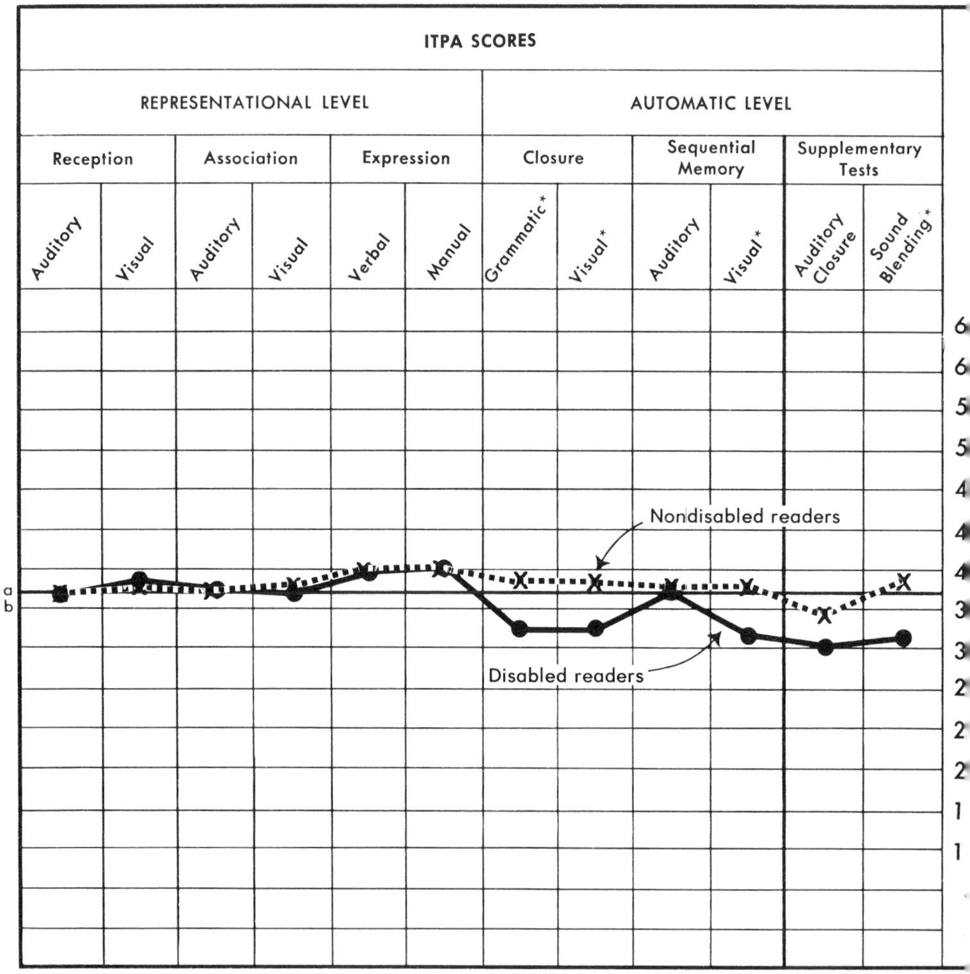

ITPA SCORES

REPRESENTATIONAL LEVEL			AUTOMATIC LEVEL		
Reception	Association	Expression	Closure	Sequential Memory	Supplementary Tests

a Mean of nondisabled reading group.   b Mean of disabled reading group.
*Significant differences between disabled and nondisabled readers were noted on these subtests ($p > .05$).

Figure 3-2

Profile of scaled scores for disabled and nondisabled readers.

Source: Macione (1969).

tests showed statistically significant differences. Auditory closure did not reach the required .05 level of significance. It is interesting to note also that there was no difference between the two groups in auditory sequential memory in Macione's study similar to the results of Kass (1966).

Other studies by Ragland (1964) and McLeod (1965) also indicate that the deficits as tested by the ITPA are primarily at the automatic level for children with reading disabilities. It appears from these studies that the automatic abilities of children are more related to reading disability than are abilities at the more symbolic or representational level.

A predictive validity study was reported by Hirshoren (1969). In this study the Stanford-Binet Intelligence Scale and the experimental edition of the ITPA were administered to forty Caucasian kindergarten children. Two years later the children were tested with the California Achievement Test (CAT). Correlations between the results of tests given in kindergarten and the second-grade achievement scores were calculated. The correlation between the Stanford-Binet and CAT total achievement score was .60; for the ITPA total language score and CAT the correlation was .72. This difference was not statistically significant. Correlations between the subtests of the ITPA and the seven tests of the CAT revealed that Visual Sequential Memory correlated the highest (from .51 with reading comprehension and .61 with reading vocabulary to .65 with spelling). For the total achievement score the correlation with Visual Sequential Memory was .71. In general, the subtests at the automatic level (Grammatic Closure, Auditory and Visual Sequential Memory) were significantly related to school achievement two years later. These results confirm the previous studies that tests at the automatic level are related to reading achievement.

Speech disorders

Ferrier (1966) and Foster (1963) conducted independent studies on the relationship of subtests of the ITPA to articulation disorders among young school children. Both Ferrier and Foster showed that this relationship also was at the automatic rather than at the representational level. Ferrier's graph, Figure 3-3, is reproduced here to show this relationship.

Children with articulatory speech defects, like the dyslexics of Kass, Ragland, and McLeod, show a deficiency in the integrational, or automatic, level with an additional deficiency in vocal encoding.

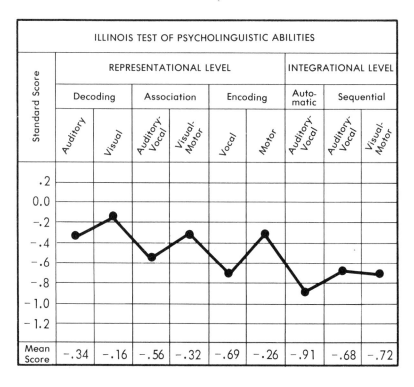

Figure 3-3

Profile of children with
articulation disorders (N = 40).

Source: Ferrier (1966).

From these studies it appears that the automatic level is more
closely related to speech defect than is the representational or symbolic level.

Mental retardation

A number of studies appear to indicate that mentally retarded
children, too, have lower scores on tests at the automatic level than
at the representational level. The deficits at the automatic level for
both mongoloid and nonmongoloid children are demonstrated quite
clearly in Figure 3-4 from the study by Jeanne McCarthy (1965)
with young day-school children and in Figures 3-13 and 3-14 from
the study by Wiseman (1965) with residential educable mentally
retarded children. These findings, especially the deficits in visual

and auditory sequential abilities, are in consonance with other findings that the mentally retarded are deficient in short-term memory.

In summarizing some of the studies on mental retardation, Bateman and Wetherell (1965) stated that there is "a typical profile for groups of retarded children whose IQ's are near or below 75. The outstanding feature is a deficit in the entire automatic level as compared to the relative strength at the representational level."

In spite of these consistent findings, the reader should be cautioned that the diagnosis of mental retardation from an individual profile is not possible, since other children with reading disabilities or articulation defects have similar deficiencies.

Mongoloid children

Two studies have been made with mongoloid children, one by David Bilovsky and Jack Share (1965) and one by Jeanne McCarthy (1965). McCarthy compared thirty mongoloid with thirty nonmongoloid children in day-school classes for trainable mentally retarded children. She found that (a) the mongoloid children were clearly superior in motor encoding in relation to their other abilities and (b) the mongoloids were superior to the nonmongoloids in motor encoding. Figure 3-4 presents the psycholinguistic profiles of the mongoloid and nonmongoloid groups of the same CA and MA. Similar findings were obtained by Bilovsky and Share (1965). They did not compare the mongoloid children with others, but found that the mongoloid children were superior in motor encoding in comparison with their other abilities.

Cerebral palsy

James J. McCarthy (1957) compared athetoid and spastic cerebral-palsied children on the Sievers Language Facility Test. His major findings included a superiority of spastic children over athetoid children at the automatic level. The athetoids were inferior to their other abilities on the automatic tests. Meyers (1963) conducted a similar study with the ITPA but used a normal group for a control. The results of her experiment are presented in Figure 3-5. It will be noted from Figure 3-5 that the normal group profile is a straight line similar to that of the standardization group. Both the athetoids and spastics were below the normal group on all subtests. The spastics show lower abilities than the athetoids on tests

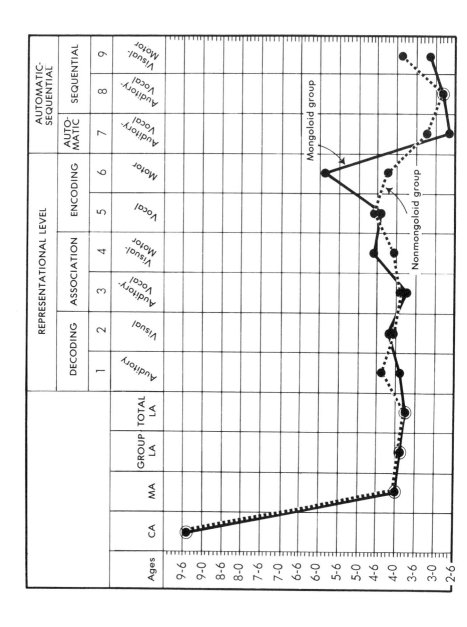

Figure 3-4

Profiles of mongoloid and nonmongoloid children.

Source: McCarthy (1965).

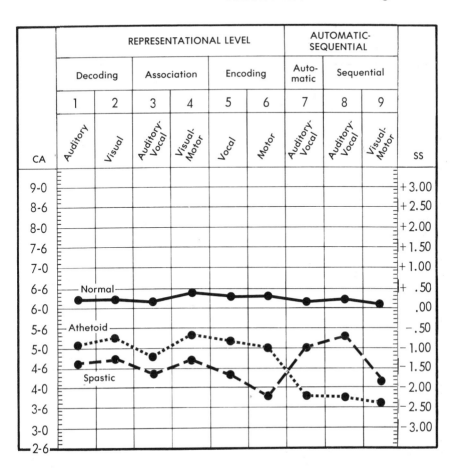

Figure 3-5

Profiles of spastic and athetoid children.

Source: Meyers (1963).

at the representational level but show a superiority to the athetoids at the automatic level.

Dillon (1966) used the ITPA to compare cerebral-palsied and noninvolved children, ages 7-9 to 10-11. He used twenty-five pairs of children matched in intelligence, age, and sex. As in Meyers's study, the cerebral-palsied children were significantly inferior to the noncerebral-palsied children on all nine subtests of the ITPA.

Ethnic groups

Ryckman (1966) studied fifty young Negro children from middle-class areas and compared them with fifty Negro children of the same age from lower socioeconomic levels. It will be noted from Figure 3-6 that the Negro children from middle-class homes show superior abilities on all subtests as compared to Negro children from lower socioeconomic homes.

It should be noted, however, that in auditory sequential memory (short-term auditory memory) both the lower- and middle-class

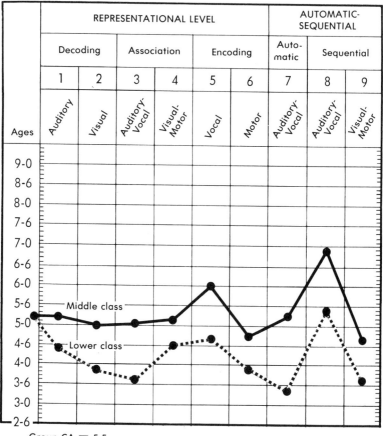

Group CA = 5-5.

Figure 3-6

Profiles of middle- and lower-class Negro children.

Source: Ryckman (1966).

Negro children show superiority over their other abilities and over that of the Caucasian standardization group. Although the lower-class Negro children scored below the standardization norms on most tests, the profile is different from the profiles shown by mentally retarded children, where the lowest part on the profile is in short-term memory.

The Ryckman study was conducted with the experimental edition of the ITPA. The revised edition has been used with Negro as well as with such other ethnic groups as Mexican Americans and Indians.

In a study, *The Impact of Head Start* (1969), Negro children were given the ten basic subtests of the revised ITPA. Figure 3-7 shows the profile for second-grade Negro children. It will be noted from the profile that this sample of Negro children, like Ryckman's sample on the experimental edition of the ITPA, shows superior ability (above their other abilities) in auditory sequential memory.

Figure 3-8 gives a profile of Mexican-American children in a Head Start program. On the revised ITPA Mexican-American children show a similar profile to Negro children, except in the two sequential memory tests. It is interesting to note that Mexican-American children do not show superiority in auditory sequential memory as do Negro children but instead appear to be superior in visual sequential memory.

Lombardi (1970) studied the psycholinguistic abilities of Papago Indian children in the first and third grades. Figure 3-9 shows the profiles of Indian children on the revised ITPA. It will be noted that the Papago Indian children were in general significantly below the standardization population in all functions except visual sequential memory. On this test the Indian children were significantly superior (at the .05 level) to the standardization population

Figure 3-7

Profile of Head Start Negro children.

Source: *Impact of Head Start* (1969).

Figure 3-8

Profile of Head Start Mexican-American children.

Source: *Impact of Head Start* (1969).

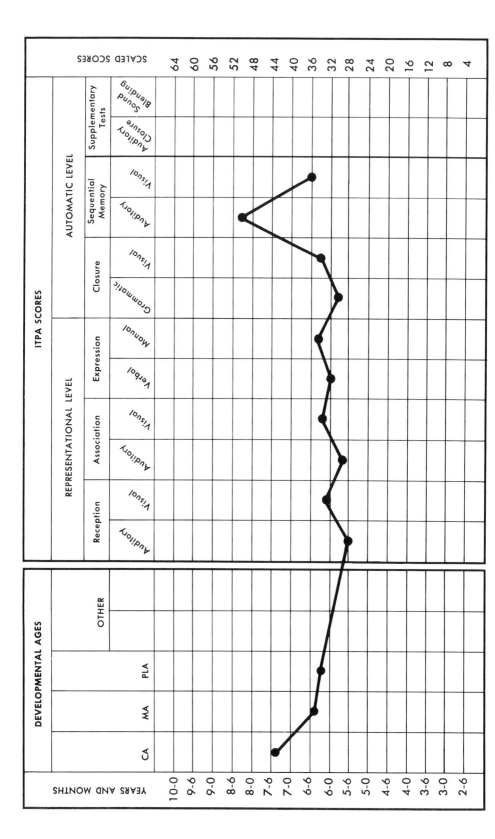

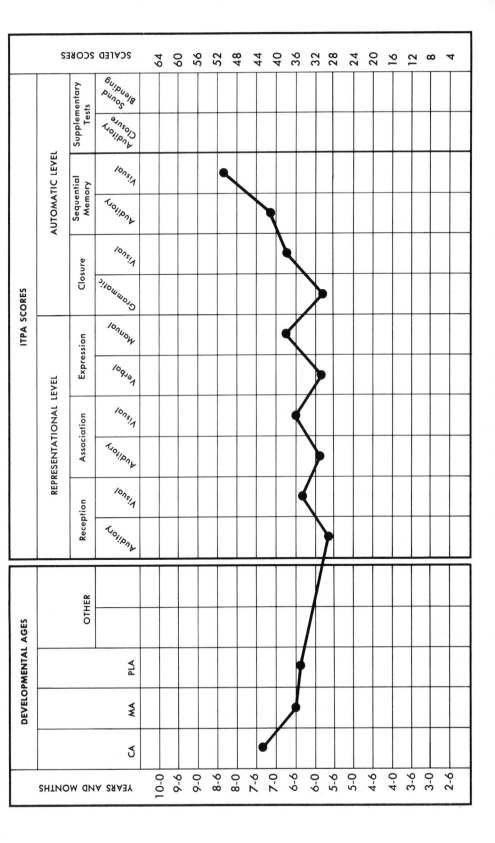

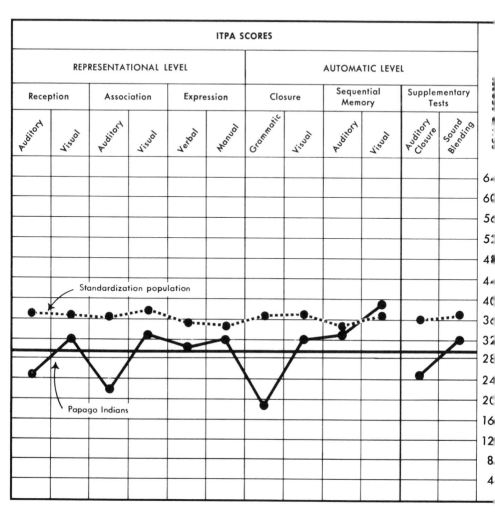

Figure 3-9

Profile of Papago Indian children.

Source: Lombardi (1970).

and to their other abilities. The profile for the Indian children with a superiority in visual sequential memory is similar to the profile of Mexican Americans. The basic deficiencies found among Indian children were in the auditory-vocal channel.

Garber (1968) administered the experimental edition of the ITPA to Navajo children. His findings also showed a superiority of visual sequential ability among Navajo Indian children.

Children with sensory handicaps

A study was conducted by Bateman (1963) on the psycholinguistic and reading functions of 131 children enrolled in twenty classes for the partially seeing in Illinois. She found that children classified as legally blind tested below the standardization population on the visual subtests. In classes for the partially seeing those children who had visual acuity greater than 20/200 showed no significant inferiority on the tests utilizing the visual-motor channel as compared with their auditory-vocal abilities. Bateman concluded that with mild and moderate visual handicaps, the ITPA measures central rather than peripheral processes, and that mild visual defects do not affect scores on ITPA subtests using the visual modality.

Olson (1960), Reichstein (1963), and Hamlin (1962) studied the effects of hearing loss on children's responses using the ITPA. Olson compared children diagnosed clinically as receptive-aphasic, expressive-aphasic, and deaf. A covariance analysis of the test results showed that the ITPA discriminates these three groups of handicapped children with communication disorders. Profiles of the deaf and the receptive-aphasic children were each consistent within their own groups. Those children diagnosed as expressive-aphasic, however, did not present a stable profile. These children appeared to be not a homogeneous group but, rather, to have a wide assortment of disabilities and abilities as measured by the ITPA. The deaf were superior to the receptive-aphasic group on the Visual-Motor Association test and on some of the auditory tests. It is likely that the deaf used their speech reading ability to interpret the auditory stimuli while the receptive-aphasics did not possess this skill, even though they both came from the same school.

Reichstein (1963) administered the ITPA to twenty-four hard-of-hearing children and twenty-four receptive-aphasic children four and a half to six and a half years of age and of approximately the same IQ. In this study the hard-of-hearing group was significantly superior to the receptive-aphasic group on all auditory and visual tests except Visual Sequential Memory and Motor Encoding. These findings on hard-of-hearing and receptive-aphasics parallel those of Olson's on deaf and receptive-aphasics.

Hamlin (1962) tested twenty-nine students attending the Kansas School for the Deaf. She found a negative correlation between the ITPA total score and the degree of hearing loss; i.e., the greater the

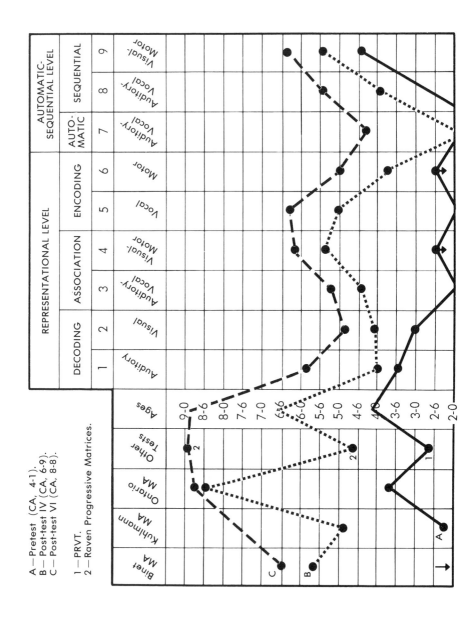

Figure 3-10

Sally's ITPA profiles.

hearing loss, the lower the score on the ITPA. Although the children in this study were twelve years old (above the age for the norms of the ITPA) and their scores on the visual tests were at the top of the norms, their auditory-channel test scores ranged from language ages of two to four years.

Effects of remediation

In 1909 Alfred Binet, having constructed the Binet-Simon Scale, published a book entitled *Modern Ideas about Children*. One of his chapters was entitled "Educability of Intelligence." In this chapter he stated that since we had now discovered the evil (mental retardation), our next step was to cure it. He then proposed that the cure for mental retardation was specific training of attention, memory, reasoning, and other faculties. He consequently organized special classes for the mentally retarded and designed curricula to develop their intelligence.

During the present century we have had numerous controversies about whether intelligence is more or less of a fixed ability and whether it is modifiable through training. The present climate indicates that intelligence, as measured by intelligence tests, can be modified somewhat through experience at early ages and through preschool education or drastic changes in home environment.

The use of the ITPA in prescribing remediation, especially for young children, may be an approach to the educability of intelligence. Below will be presented some evidence from case studies as well as from group studies on the effects of remediation.

Three case studies

1. *Sally.* Figure 3-10 shows three profiles obtained over a period of four years for a girl who was diagnosed as severely mentally retarded. This case has been reported in detail elsewhere (Kirk, 1966). Only a summary will be given here.

At the age of seven months Sally had been hospitalized because of her inability to eat, malnutrition, and poor general development. Up to the age of four she had not learned to talk. She had been examined in several pediatric and neurological clinics, the diagnosis having been mental retardation, a possible atonic diplegia, and/or a possible apraxia. Examining physicians felt there was a cerebral dysfunction but were unable to find definitive neurological evidence. At the age of four she spoke no words and uttered few sounds.

At the age of four Profile A of Figure 3-10 was obtained. It will be noted that on the Stanford-Binet Sally's mental age was below two years. She obtained an IQ of 56 on the Kuhlmann Tests of Mental Development and an IQ of 90 on the Ontario School Ability Examination (a performance test of intelligence for deaf children). On the ITPA she demonstrated average ability in visual sequential memory and in auditory decoding. In visual decoding ability she was only one year retarded. She could not score on any of the other subtests of the ITPA.

Since psychometric and psycholinguistic tests on Sally showed wide discrepancies in growth, it seemed wise to consider her a child with a learning disability instead of mentally retarded. Speech and expressive language, both vocal and motor, were her major areas of deficit.

Initial tutoring sessions emphasized oral response. Later she was tutored in her home for several years in an attempt to develop speech and language ability. Because of her relatively superior visual sequencing ability, she was taught to read sentences and to respond to oral questions, first by reading the answer (visual cue), then by a response to the question without reading. She was consequently aided in language and speech through reading. It will be noted from Profile B (Figure 3-10) that her mental age from year four until year 6-9 increased significantly on both verbal and nonverbal intelligence tests. Her ITPA profile showed similar gains except for vocal encoding. Because of her rapid development as shown on intelligence tests as well as on the ITPA, she was not placed in a special class for the mentally retarded but was given a second year of kindergarten and then placed in the regular first grade at the age of 6-6.

Profile C in Figure 3-10 was obtained when she was in the third grade at age 8-9, after two years of school without individual tutoring. As will be noted from Profile C, she continued to develop mentally and psycholinguistically but not at the same rate as earlier. From age four to age eight she progressed one year for each year in both mental age and psycholinguistic development, and was reading only slightly below the expectation for her CA. She showed continuous development on the ITPA, in mental age, and in educational achievement. Although she was not of average ability, we cannot classify this girl as mentally retarded. She has progressed to the eighth grade and is doing acceptable work.

2. *William.* William was first examined at the age of 4-7 be-

cause he had been excluded from a nursery school for disruptive and immature behavior. This boy had been delayed in development in both talking and walking. According to his mother he used very few words at fifteen months of age and did not talk in two-word sentences until thirty-five months. He crawled at eighteen months and walked at twenty-three months. The physical examination at age four was negative, although the physician noted delayed motor coordination.

Figure 3-11 shows three profiles of William's abilities: at age 4-7, before tutoring (A); at age 6-1, after tutoring (B); and at age 6-10, after a change of tutoring (C) to be described later. At age 4-7 William obtained a mental age of 3-6 and an IQ of 79 on the Stanford-Binet. On the Peabody Picture Vocabulary Test he obtained a mental age of 4-3 and an IQ of 97. On the ITPA he showed marked deficiencies in visual sequencing, motor and vocal encoding, and visual and auditory association. His other psycholinguistic abilities were within the normal range.

William was tutored between the ages of 4-8 and 6-1 and was also enrolled in a kindergarten at age 5-2. The initial stages of tutoring emphasized motor encoding and visual sequential memory activities. Later, visual-motor association activities were integrated with motor encoding and visual sequencing tasks (see Kirk, 1966, for greater details of stages in tutoring). Profile B of Figure 3-11 shows the progress that was made in areas of deficit over a period of one and a half years. Motor and vocal encoding and visual and auditory association showed over two to four years' progress during this period.

Between the ages of 6-1 and 6-10 William continued in kindergarten. He was not tutored during the first semester but during the second semester, in addition to individual tutoring, he was placed in a special group. This program consisted of recreational games designed especially to integrate seeing and hearing (visual with auditory decoding), seeing or hearing and doing (visual or auditory decoding with motor encoding), seeing or hearing and saying (visual or auditory decoding with vocal encoding), and doing and saying (vocal with motor encoding) (see Painter, 1966, for details).

Profile C of Figure 3-11 shows marked improvement of decoding and encoding ability in both visual-motor and auditory-vocal channels. The performance on these functions of the ITPA was, at the time of the final examination, from one to over two years in excess

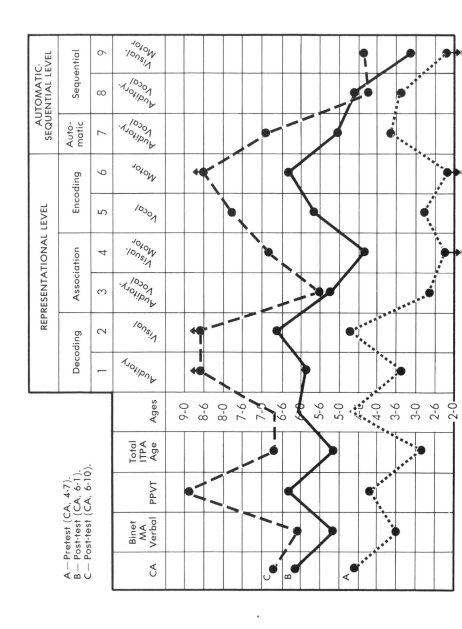

Figure 3-11

William's ITPA profiles.

of the chronological age of 6-10. The functions of auditory and visual sequencing, not stressed during this remedial period, did not show significant improvement. It was interesting to note also that on the Peabody Picture Vocabulary Test, involving as it does visual and auditory decoding, the mental age at age 6-10 was 8-11, and the IQ on this test was 120. On the Stanford-Binet the mental age was 6-0 and the IQ was 86. On the latter William's mental age had improved twenty-five months in a period of twenty-six months.

3. *John*. John was referred at the age of ten as a child who did not talk spontaneously. He was noncommunicative and undemonstrative. No emotional or biological reason was found which would explain this boy's unwillingness or inability to express himself. When called upon directly and asked a question demanding a "yes" or "no" answer, or if the question could be answered with a one-word response, he usually answered readily. The teacher reported that in class he would raise his hand to answer a question or discuss a problem, but when called upon he would stand and look expressionless.

Group Intelligence Tests, the Raven Progressive Matrices, and the WISC gave him IQs well above 100. The only test on which he scored low was the Goodenough Draw-a-Man Test, on which he obtained an IQ of 73. Educationally he was performing at the third grade in reading although placed in the fourth grade. Cursive writing was illegible. Counselors and speech correctionists attempted to help him with little success.

Figure 3-12 presents John's profile on the experimental edition of the ITPA. It will be noted from Profile A that John scored near the top of the norms in all functions except encoding or expression. In this ability he was severely defective in both verbal and manual expression.

Observations of this boy confirmed the results of the ITPA. He did not express himself verbally or manually. He could memorize a fourteen-line poem and recite it from memory but could not express a single idea of the poem verbally or in writing. He appeared to know answers to questions but was unable to structure and express the ideas verbally or manually.

The remedial program for this boy has been described by Kirk (1966). The program outlined to improve John's verbal encoding (expression) and motor encoding (expression) was programmed with materials that were self-paced. A typewriter and a tape recorder were used for frames produced by a computer. Incomplete

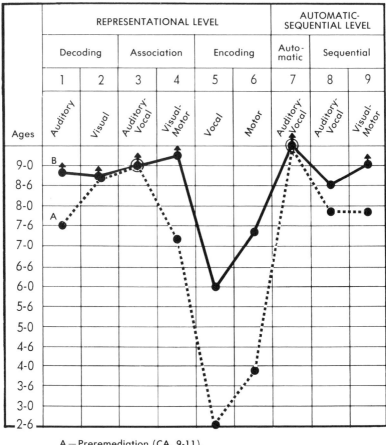

A — Preremediation (CA, 9-11).
B — Postremediation (CA, 10-10).

Figure 3-12

John's ITPA profiles.

sentences were presented to him on the typewriter. He was required to complete the sentence, read it, then hear what he read. The printout from the computer consisted of sheets of paper on which actual frames of a program were typed, three frames on each sheet. Initially a sentence might be simply, "The ball is roun—." The boy was required to fill in the "d," then roll up the sheet to the verification printed below. A later sentence would be "The —— is ——," or "A rou—, pur— thing often is a grape." The computer produced sentences where more and more of the prompting materials were omitted (vanished).

In this program the typewriter provided a simple form of motor encoding. The tape recorder provided John with a feedback on his verbal reading expression of the sentence. In brief, the systematic programmed lessons provided for (a) motor encoding exercises (typing), (b) verbal encoding (reading the completed sentences), (c) confirmation (his response and the correct answer), (d) self-administration, (e) self-determined performance standards, (f) performance-dependent step sizes, and (g) a closely structured program.

The results of seven months of tutoring, three hours a week, are presented in Figure 3-12, Profile B. It will be noted that significant progress was made in both verbal and motor encoding. One year after the program was initiated and six months after tutoring ceased, an evaluation was made. The homeroom teacher reported that John now answered questions readily. His answers increased in length during the year. He was participating in group discussions and in charades (motor encoding) with his classmates. He was no longer considered "the boy who doesn't talk."

The three case studies reported above are examples of a substantial number of idiographic studies which have been accumulated (Kirk, 1966). Individual cases have been treated and tested prior to and following remediation. Practically all of these reports show substantial improvement in the areas of deficit in the children studied. Improvement on tests has also been reflected in reports of improvement in the home and in the school.

Group studies

In addition to a considerable number of case studies showing beneficial effects of remediation on learning deficits, there have been reported a number of studies using experimental and control groups: Smith (1962), Hart (1963), and Wiseman (1965).

In each of these studies matched groups were used to examine the effects of remediation on psycholinguistic development. In each instance significant gains in psycholinguistic skills were made by experimental groups in comparison with the controls. Only one of these studies will be reported here.

Wiseman (1965) tutored an experimental group of ten educable mentally retarded children who had been chosen at random from ten pairs of boys matched in disabilities. Boys in the experimental group were tutored individually for a six-month period and compared to the control group which attended the same classes but did not receive tutoring in their areas of deficit. Figure 3-13 shows the pre- and post-tests for the experimental group while Figure 3-14 shows the results on the same tests for the control group. The experimental group showed substantial and significant gains in their areas of deficit, the areas emphasized during the tutoring sessions, but no significant gains in their areas of asset. The control group, however, made no significant gains in any area during the same period.

It might well be argued that there is nothing very remarkable about teaching children the skills measured by a test and then discovering that their scores on that test improve. The crucial question is whether there is any positive transfer effect to performance in other areas. Whereas coaching to obtain an increase in IQ has had no significant effect on the educational growth of children, there *are* indications of positive transfer from the remediation of psycholinguistic disabilities to reading and perhaps to intelligence. In a small but well-controlled experiment in Australia, Hart (1963) found that his experimental group of cerebral-palsied children responded to psycholinguistic remediation not only by showing considerable improvement in ITPA performance but also by achieving a significantly higher reading level at the end of the period of remediation, despite the fact that they had had no special tutoring in reading itself.

Summary and discussion

Selected research studies using the experimental edition and the revised edition have been reported. These studies have been restricted to investigations of characteristics of different groups of children and on the effects of remediation. This research leads to the following generalizations:

1. Reading disability cases (dyslexics) tend to have superior abilities at the conceptual or representational level as compared to their abilities at the automatic level, including grammatic closure and auditory and visual short-term memory. This raises the question of the trainability of these psychological functions and the effect of early training in perceptual speed, closure, and visual and auditory sequential memory in preventing reading disabilities. It appears from these studies that remediation for children with reading disabilities has to be related to the training of functions at the automatic level. Breaking the code, as Chall (1967) calls it, may mean developing the automatic level.

2. Mentally retarded children appear to be superior in representational functions as compared to their abilities at the nonsymbolic (or automatic) level. Studies which have been made with the ITPA confirm other experimental studies on the deficiency in short-term memory of the mentally retarded. These findings apply equally to educable mentally retarded, mongoloid, and nonmongoloid trainable mentally retarded children.

3. Mongoloid children show a superiority in motor encoding as compared to vocal encoding and other psycholinguistic abilities. The mongoloids are also superior in motor encoding when compared with nonmongoloids of the same chronological and mental age. In this connection it should be recalled that Luria (1963) has stated that mental defect represents a dissociation of the two aspects of the second signal system, the vocal and the motor. Since in our studies only the mongoloids appear to show a significant discrepancy between vocal and motor expressive abilities, it is possible to conjecture that Luria's hypothesis applies only to mongoloids.

4. Normal children with articulatory speech defects appear to have the same disabilities on the ITPA as reading cases and the mentally retarded, namely, a deficiency in the automatic level. They also show a deficiency in vocal encoding on the ITPA.

5. Spastic cerebral-palsied children tend to be inferior to athetoid cerebral-palsied children in psycholinguistic functions at the representational level. The status is reversed at the automatic level, where the spastics are superior to the athetoids. The latter show a marked deficiency, like the mentally retarded and reading disability cases, in grammatic closure and auditory and visual sequential memory.

6. There appears to be a significant difference in ethnic groups in auditory and visual sequential memory. Young middle-class Negro children show a normal profile on all psycholinguistic abilities except in auditory sequential memory. In the latter these Negro children are superior to their other abilities and also superior to the standardization population. Lower-class Negro children show deficiencies on psycholinguistic functions as compared to both the standardization population and middle-class Negro children. The one exception is again in auditory sequential memory, in which lower-class Negro children are superior to their other abilities,

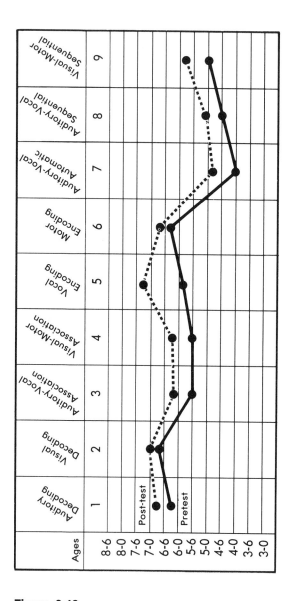

Figure 3-13

Pre- and post-test profiles of an experimental group
of educable mentally retarded children.

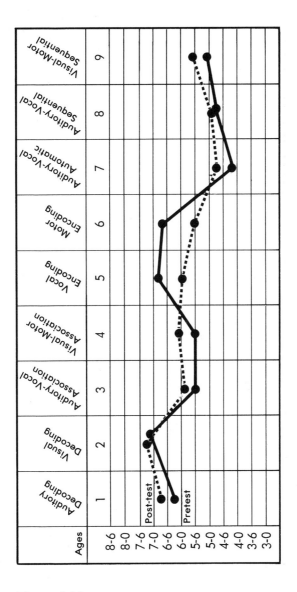

Figure 3-14

Pre- and post-test profiles of a control group
of educable mentally retarded children.

Source: Wiseman (1965).

equal to the normative group, but still inferior to young middle-class Negro children.

Mexican-American children differ from both Negro and Caucasian children. Mexican-American children appear to have average abilities in auditory sequential memory but a superior ability in visual sequential memory. Studies on Indian children show two differentiating characteristics. One is a superiority to both Negroes and Caucasians (like Mexican Americans) in visual sequential memory. In addition, Indian children are deficient in the auditory-vocal channel as compared to the visual-motor channel, and as compared to middle-class Negroes and Caucasians. The differences in auditory and visual memory among different ethnic groups may indicate that there are some differentiating factors in their early training.

7. As would be expected, legally blind children show inferiority in the visual-motor channel as compared to their auditory-vocal channel functioning. On the other hand, partially seeing children not diagnosed as legally blind do not show this inferiority. These findings lead to the conclusion that with children having visual acuity better than 20/200, the ITPA is testing central rather than peripheral processes.

8. Studies on hearing-defective and sensory-aphasic children indicate that the deaf and hard-of-hearing perform at a higher level on tests utilizing the auditory channel than do sensory-aphasics.

9. Remediation of children's disabilities found by the ITPA presents encouraging results. Idiographic as well as nomothetic research in this area points to the conclusion that different disabilities identified by the ITPA can be ameliorated through systematic remedial programs. Programs emphasizing the training of psycholinguistic disabilities with disadvantaged preschool children have shown promising results (Karnes, 1968; Karnes et al., 1969).

The ITPA, along with other diagnostic tests that have been or are being developed, represents a new approach to the management of children with learning disabilities—diagnosis of children's cognitive, linguistic, and perceptual abilities for the purpose of remediation—in contrast to assessment for the purpose of classification or categorization.

Chapter four

The
diagnostic
process

O ne of the problems that has retarded the development of diagnostic-remedial programs in schools is the customary "division of
labor" between school psychologists and remedial teachers. Schools
have in the past required psychologists to administer psychometric
tests (such as the Stanford-Binet or WISC) for the purpose of
placement of children in special classes or special groups rather
than assessment of the child in such a way as to assist the teacher in
organizing an appropriate remedial program. School psychologists
in many instances felt that their responsibility was ended when they
labeled the child and recommended placement in a particular
group.

Teachers, on the other hand, were responsible for organizing
the educational program for the children placed in their classes by
the psychologist. The program a teacher evolved resulted from her
assessment of the child and generally had little relationship to the
work of the psychologist.

What is needed in the field of learning disabilities is a diagnostic-
remedial program, beginning with an assessment of the child in
terms of his abilities and disabilities and proceeding to an appropriate remedial program. Perhaps these two responsibilities should
be incorporated in a single diagnostic-remedial teacher, one who

is the responsible agent for scientific assessment as well as appropriate remediation. If such a highly trained individual is not available, there should be close coordination and mutual understanding of goals and procedures between the diagnostician and the remedial teacher. Diagnosis should lead to remediation and the remediation procedures should be developed in the light of the diagnostic hypothesis.

The diagnostic process that leads to a program of remediation generally follows five stages: (a) determining whether a learning problem exists, (b) determining the behavior manifestations and the specific problems encountered by the child, (c) discovering the physical, environmental, and psychological correlates of the disability, (d) evolving a diagnostic hypothesis on the basis of the behavioral analysis and the correlates, and (e) organizing a systematic remedial program based on the symptoms and deficits and diagnostic hypotheses determined during the previous stages. The stages are described in more detail below.

Determining that a problem exists

The first step that must be accomplished is to determine whether a specific learning problem exists. For example, if a child is in the third grade and has not learned to read, a general intelligence test is given to determine whether or not he has the capacity to read. If the child's IQ is found to be 50, one would infer that the child is mentally retarded and is not expected to read at the age of eight. On the other hand, if the child has average intelligence, has learned arithmetic, seems to have relatively normal language ability, is in the third grade, and still has not learned to read beyond the primer level, then a learning problem in reading possibly exists. But there may be other reasons that he has not learned to read. It is possible that the child has a sensory handicap or he may be emotionally disturbed and hence has not learned to read by ordinary methods. These factors must also be discovered before one can determine whether a specific learning disability exists. The major task at this stage is to be able to define the problem. In this particular case the child is of average intelligence, has learned to do arithmetic computation not requiring reading, appears to have adequate language ability for his age, is not severely emotionally disturbed, deaf, or blind. In this initial stage we have determined that the boy's problem is a specific reading disability.

The data which have led to the determination of a specific reading disability are:

Chronological age	8-4
Mental age	8-2
Arithmetic computational age	7-8
Reading age	6-3

In this case we have a discrepancy between chronological age, mental age, and arithmetic achievement age on the one hand and level of reading on the other hand. It is assumed here that the child has attended school with fair regularity, has had adequate teaching for two years, and has still not learned to read.

In another instance the child may be five years old and have not learned to talk. We know that children with marked mental retardation may have retarded speech or language at the age of five. However, if we are able to exclude the diagnosis of mental retardation, or deafness, or other factors that might interfere with the development of language, then we define the child's problem as delay in learning to talk as a result of some specific learning disability.

In either case the decision that a specific learning disability exists is determined by the amount of discrepancy between the capacity to perform and the actual development or achievement in reading, talking, listening, thinking, perceiving, etc.

Determining the symptoms
by behavioral analysis and description
of the disability

The second stage of the diagnostic remedial process is to make a behavioral analysis of the child, a determination of *how* he reads instead of his level of reading. This stage is best illustrated in the field of reading where observations or diagnostic tests are given to determine faulty reading habits. Here we might find that the child lacks word attack skills, has excessive errors such as reversals, vowels, or slow speed of reading, does not use context clues, omits sounds and words, makes substitutions, and so forth. Such observations can be made by listening to a child read if the examiner is skilled in diagnosing such disabilities, or diagnostic reading tests may be used to determine the major difficulties in learning to read. In certain situations these errors or poor habits in reading can be observed and noted.

A child may be five years old and not have learned to talk at the level of a five-year-old. Observations must be made of his speech, use of syntax, sentence length in talking, response to auditory or visual inputs, and other factors relating to speech and language. One must exclude severe mental retardation, hearing loss, and emotional factors. If these do not exist to any noticeable degree, then a learning disability exists.

The correlates of disabilities

In the past considerable energy has been expended in an effort to find the cause (etiology) of a disability. This is an outgrowth of medical procedure in which it is futile to treat a symptom which will only recur if the basic cause is not eradicated. The physician does not treat a fever as a basic problem but as a symptom caused by a virus or other fever-producing agent. On the other hand, when the causative factor is irremediable the symptom must be treated as such or circumvented. If a hand has been amputated, the manual incapacity must be circumvented and the use of other parts of the body must be developed.

With learning disabilities, wherever there is an ongoing cause such as poor auditory reception due to a hearing loss, or emotional upsets due to traumatic family conditions, or neurological malfunction due to a brain tumor, it goes without saying that the cause should be eradicated if at all possible. The effort to discover causes is therefore important for the prevention of disability, but in most cases the cause, be it brain damage or genetic malfunctioning, is not something which can be treated and eliminated.

If, for example, a child who has not learned to speak, read, discriminate sounds, or perceive visually is found to have an abnormal EEG, it is inferred that the brain dysfunction is the cause of his disability. But brain dysfunction, not remediable at our present stage of scientific knowledge, and the finding of the abnormal EEG, though valuable, do not have much relationship to remediation or the organization of a remedial program. Some of the symptoms of the brain dysfunction, such as hyperkinesis or distractability or perseveration or emotional instability, may determine certain remedial procedures, but these conditions, not the presence of a brain lesion, determine the methods used. In such cases it is the symptoms which are dealt with, not the cause; for, after all, the cause-and-effect relationships among the various anomalies of learning disabilities are not always clear-cut and simple. Does a child have regressive eye movements in reading because he reads poorly, or does he read poorly because he has regressive eye movements?

It is for this reason that the term "correlates" is used instead of "causes," since the emphasis here will be primarily on educational correlates or factors relating to the functional behavior of the child. A child who is unable to learn words may have a sound blending disability. This is considered a correlate of inability to learn to read, and leads to a remedial program which will include training the child's sound blending in relation to teaching him to read.

The search for correlates of a learning disability is a search for related factors within the child or his environment which have been found to occur frequently with the disability under consideration and which need correction or amelioration. These correlates may be (a) physical factors, (b) environmental factors, or (c) psychological factors:

Physical Correlates	*Environmental Correlates*	*Psychological Correlates*
Visual defects	Traumatic experiences	Poor visual or auditory perception and discrimination
Auditory defects	Conditioned avoidance reactions	Slow understanding and interpretation of concepts
Confused spatial orientation	Undue family pressures	
Mixed laterality	Bilingualism	Poor organizing and generalizing ability
Hyperkinesis	Sensory deprivation	Inability to express concepts
Poor body image	Lack of school experience	Minimal motor and verbal skills
Undernourishment		Poor short-term memory
		Poor closure

The major purpose of developing the ITPA was to be able to discover psychological correlates of different learning disabilities. The efficient diagnostician will seek other tests not included in the ITPA which may uncover relevant correlates that can be remediated.

The diagnostic hypothesis

In a sense the diagnostic hypothesis is one of the most important factors in diagnosis. This consists of a summary of the symptoms and the correlates that have inhibited the child's learning to talk, read, write, or spell. This requires experienced clinicians who can use the relevant tests, select the relevant facts, and put the pieces together in organized form so as to explain the child's inability to learn. The diagnostic hypothesis must select the relevant variables in the case and pinpoint the specific disabilities upon which the remedial program can be organized.

To illustrate, a case may be cited. Ralph was in the fourth grade at the age of 9-7. He was referred because he had, up to that point, been unable to learn to read. He had been promoted each year since the first grade because he had acquired considerable information and was doing fourth-grade arithmetic. On the WISC he obtained an IQ of 140. On several reading tests he scored middle or high first grade. By observing his attempts to read, it was obvious that he recognized a few words, guessed from the context in oral reading, but had no method of word attack. The home and school environments were more than adequate.

An analysis of psychological correlates indicated superior ability in most psychological functions. Two major disabilities were noted. First, on visual sequential memory tests he scored very low. Informal tests of visual memory, such as asking him to write a word like "horse" from memory after it had been written on the board by the examiner, confirmed the test results. He could not remember and reproduce what he saw. Second, he had a severe disability in sound blending, being unable to blend two or three sounds such as "sh–oe," or "c–a–t." Checking for physical correlates, it was found that he had visual fusion problems and a possible eye-muscle imbalance. An examination by an ophthalmologist later revealed an exophoria. Hearing and auditory discrimination were normal. From these data a diagnostic hypothesis was evolved: this boy's inability to learn to read appeared to be affected by his inability to remember consistently what he saw (visual sequential memory). His poor visual memory may have been related to poor visual fusion which in turn may have been affected by the eye-muscle imbalance. The reading disability might have been compensated for if he had used auditory methods to aid him in reading, but auditory methods were not effective because of his disability in sound blending.

With this diagnostic hypothesis the remedial program in reading was obvious: correct the exophoria as much as possible and train the visual sequential memory through writing words and phrases from memory. He was required to look at a word, then erase the word and write it from memory as many times as was needed to reproduce it correctly. At the same time his sound blending ability was trained by the method described in Chapter 9. Remedial reading focused on the correction or amelioration of his physical and psychological disabilities through the medium of reading materials. The remedial procedure was so successful that this boy attained sufficient academic achievement to graduate from college.

Organizing a remedial program

As indicated earlier, the organization of the remedial program depends upon the diagnostic hypothesis. It is of little value in a specific case to ascribe a reading disability to multiple factors. It is important to isolate these factors or correlates, find the relationships, and organize the remedial program in harmony with these relationships. The remedial program should attempt to ameliorate the psychological deficiencies in relation to the major problem. If a child has a significant deficiency in visual sequential memory which has retarded his ability to learn to spell, visual sequential memory should be trained directly with letters and words rather than in isolation with diamonds, squares, and triangles.

If a child does not talk in sentences and has a marked deficiency in auditory sequential memory, teaching auditory memory should be trained directly in exercises with sentences and meaningful sequences of words or games utilizing practical material. Suggestions for remedial programs are elaborated in Chapters 8 and 9.

Chapter five

Interpreting
ITPA
scores

A remedial program cannot be organized from a global test score. Such global scores as a psycholinguistic quotient, an MA, an IQ, a reading or arithmetic grade equivalent, or a percentile rank have limited value in the organization of remedial programs. To arrive at an appropriate method of instruction for a child it is necessary to make a detailed analysis of abilities and disabilities and to relate these to a program of learning for the particular child. Two complementary approaches to this procedure have evolved. One involves diagnostic testing of special functions as is done with the ITPA, which examines ten basic psycholinguistic functions, and/or with such other tests as the Frostig Tests of Visual Perception, which make an analysis of visual perceptual functions.

Another approach uses a functional analysis of a child's behavior by observing him frequently or over an extended period to determine what behavior is typical for him and what behavior needs modification. This is a "baseline" and is the level at which the remedial procedures begin. Using tangible as well as intangible rewards to reinforce the desired behavior, the remedial teacher takes the child step by step toward the proposed goal.

Both of these approaches require a rational system of diagnosis parallel to and in tune with a rational system of remediation. Behavior analysts believe that observing many samples of a child's behavior during task performance provides a more valid description of the child's ability than does formal testing. The rational system of diagnosis is important here as well as in the testing procedure. In both approaches (testing functions and functional analysis of behavior) the rational system of diagnosis is what is important. In the past most testing procedures have not followed this rational system of diagnosis and have therefore gathered irrelevant data. However, when the testing procedure follows a relevant and rational system, then relevant and rational material is gathered and the remediation may proceed along parallel lines.

Reference has been made to the complementary nature of behavior analysis and diagnostic testing and it is clear that the two approaches can work hand in hand. Since open-ended observation may range over a wide variety of functions in the child, it is believed that functional analysis of the child's behavior can be more efficiently made after diagnostic testing. Concentration can be given to those areas shown by diagnostic testing to need more careful evaluation and baseline determination. It is at this point that stimulus events, response behaviors, contingency systems, and consequent events can be analyzed. For example, if a child is found on the ITPA to perform in most areas within normal limits but performs at a lower level on, let us say, manual expression, then we would observe the child, question the teacher, check the history for information on this deficit and related activities so as to analyze his functioning in this field, and prepare the remedial program accordingly. Many of the techniques of programmed learning are appropriate for such a program.

It should also be pointed out that functional analysis of behavior plays a unique role in evaluating and modifying aberrations in social behavior while discrete diagnostic tests are used primarily in the analysis of linguistic, cognitive, and perceptual abilities. If a child bites his nails or sucks his thumb, cognitive tests are of little value. On the other hand, if a child is unable to learn to read, it is necessary to find the correlates of his inability to learn which may be deficiencies in auditory closure, sound blending, visual and auditory short-term memory, or other functions. These deficits are not readily observed, since the observation relates to the end result —that is, he cannot read. The most effective approach to diagnostic analysis is through tests to pinpoint the specific areas which can then be subjected to functional analysis if needed. In either event the teacher, utilizing the diagnostic analysis, evolves a remedial program in which she can evaluate and select stimulus events in the form of appropriate materials and utilize contingencies, reinforcements, programmed learning, and other behavior modification techniques.

The Summary Sheet of the ITPA

In the following sections an attempt is made to provide the diagnostician with guidelines for interpreting various scores and profiles obtained on the Illinois Test of Psycholinguistic Abilities.

After the ITPA has been administered and scored, the test data are recorded on the Summary Sheet in the Record Form. Figure 5-1 shows the Summary Sheet for a child of six years, four months. This sheet provides space for raw scores, psycholinguistic ages, and scaled scores for each of the subtests as well as the more global scores indicated across the bottom of the page. It is assumed that the diagnostician using the present book is also conversant with the information provided in the *Examiner's Manual* of the ITPA (Kirk, McCarthy, and Kirk, 1968) and in *The Development and Psychometric Characteristics of the Revised Illinois Test of Psycholinguistic Abilities* (Paraskevopoulos and Kirk, 1969).

The scores discussed below either appear directly on the Summary Sheet or can be derived therefrom and summarized on the page in the Record Form reserved for examiner's comments. We are interested in global scores, part scores, individual subtest scores, and the graphic representation of these provided in the Profile of Abilities.

Global scores

There are several ways of indicating the overall ability of a child from the scores obtained from the ITPA. These will be discussed in the following paragraphs.

Composite psycholinguistic age (composite PLA)

The composite PLA is derived from the "Sum of Raw Scores" on the Summary Sheet by means of Table 3 in the *Examiner's Manual*. In this case the "Composite PLA" of 5-10 indicates that the child is functioning at a level six months below his chronological age of 6-4. This PLA is a global score, an overall index of *level* of psycholinguistic development.

The composite PLA expresses the child's performance in years

| SUBTEST | REPRESENTATIONAL LEVEL | | | | | | AUTOMATIC LEVEL | | | | | |
| | AUDITORY-VOCAL | | | VISUAL-MOTOR | | | AUDITORY-VOCAL | | | VISUAL-MOTOR | | |
	Raw Score	Age Score	Scaled Score	Raw Score	Age Score	Scaled Score	Raw Score	Age Score	Scaled Score	Raw Score	Age Score	Scaled Score
AUDITORY RECEPTION	18	4-10	28									
VISUAL RECEPTION				21	6-7	38						
VISUAL MEMORY										21	7-10	42
AUDITORY ASSOCIATION	14	4-9	22									
AUDITORY MEMORY							14	4-2	27			
VISUAL ASSOCIATION				25	7-7	42						
VISUAL CLOSURE										21	6-6	37
VERBAL EXPRESSION	16	5-2	30									
GRAMMATIC CLOSURE							11	5-0	25			
MANUAL EXPRESSION				28	8-8	43						
(Supplementary tests) AUDITORY CLOSURE							13	4-11	27			
SOUND BLENDING							9	5-3	30			

SUMMARY SCORES:

Sum of Raw Scores: 189
Composite PLA: 5-10
Sum of SS: 334
Mean SS: 33
Median SS: 33.5

and months and has the advantage of using units of measurement comparable to those used in such other tests as achievement tests, which report results in educational ages, and intelligence tests, which report mental ages. Instructional materials are also frequently keyed to age levels or comparable grade levels and teachers usually evaluate a child correspondingly. Age scores are therefore more easily communicated to teachers than are more sophisticated forms of derived scores. It should be remembered, however, that age scores do not take into account the differences in variance occurring from test to test and from age to age and therefore cannot always be compared directly.

Psycholinguistic quotient (PLQ)

The psycholinguistic quotient (PLQ) does not appear on the Summary Sheet. It is derived by dividing the composite PLA by the chronological age (PLA ÷ CA = PLQ). It is a global score which indicates the *rate* (rather than the *level*) of overall psycholinguistic development. Its use is limited primarily to classification or comparison with other children. Like other global and composite scores, it has little value in organizing a remedial program. For the child shown in Figure 5-1, the PLQ would be 5-10 ÷ 6-4 = 92.

It should be noted that this score is a ratio quotient parallel to a ratio IQ derived by similar arithmetic. The WISC IQs and the 1960 Stanford-Binet IQs are deviation IQs which take into account differences in variance and can more safely be compared from age to age. If a deviation score is desired, the scaled scores discussed next should be used.

Scaled scores

It will be noted from the Summary Sheet (Figure 5-1) that a scaled score is recorded for each of the subtests. These are transformations of the raw scores such that a scaled score of 36 (with a standard deviation of 6) indicates the mean performance of each and any age group of the referral population on each of the twelve subtests. These scores are therefore comparable to each other; the scaled score for any subtest at any age can be directly compared to any other.

The *mean scaled score* is the average of the scaled scores on the ten basic subtests. It provides a reference point with which scores on individual subtests may be compared. For the child presented in Figure 5-1, the scaled scores on the ten basic subtests add up to 334; dividing this by 10, the mean scaled score is 33. This is within the range of 36 ± 6, indicating within average ability.

The *median scaled score* is derived by calculating the median of the ten basic subtests. In the present case this turns out to be 33.5. In most instances the mean scaled score is used for comparative purposes, but when discrepant subtest scores are either all above or all below the mean, it is advisable to use the median scaled score instead of the mean scaled score.

Estimated Stanford-Binet mental age

The estimated Stanford-Binet mental age is obtained from Table 4 of the second printing of the *Examiner's Manual* or from Table D of the appendix in Paraskevopoulos and Kirk (1969). The data in this table were derived from the scores of the standardization group since the Stanford-Binet Scale, Form L-M, had been administered to the 962 children in the normative group. It was thus possible to ascertain the relationship between the composite raw score on the ITPA and the Stanford-Binet mental age. These MAs were obtained by plotting mean mental ages against mean raw scores for the eight age groups of the normative population. These eight points were then smoothed to form a curve from which estimated mental age on the horizontal axis could be read from a raw score on the vertical axis. These data were then included in the second printing of the *Examiner's Manual* (1970).

For the child presented in Figure 5-1, the estimated Stanford-Binet mental age derived from his raw score of 189 was 6-0.

Estimated Stanford-Binet IQ

To obtain an estimated Binet IQ the estimated Stanford-Binet MA derived above is applied to the Pinneau Revised IQ Tables (Terman and Merrill, 1960). For the present case, the estimated MA of 6-0 and the CA of 6-4 result in an IQ of 94. The estimated Stanford-Binet MA and IQ should be considered only as approximations.

Part scores

The scores thus far discussed (composite PLA, PLQ, mean and median scaled scores, and estimated Binet scores) are all global scores and have limited value. The common use is for interindividual comparisons. More discriminating scores can be derived by considering the child's abilities in each of the three dimensions which the ITPA measures, i.e., his scores in the auditory-vocal channel as compared to his scores in the visual-motor channel, or his scores representing each of the two levels of organization or each of the three processes.

It will be noted that the Summary Sheet is set up to make such comparisons easy. The major page is divided according to level, with the tests at the representational level at the left and the tests at the automatic level at the right. Thus a part score on the first six tests (those at the representational level) can be compared with the part score on the last four tests (those at the automatic level).

Similarly, all of the auditory-vocal tests in columns 1 and 3 can be compared with all of the visual-motor tests in columns 2 and 4.

In comparing scores among the three processes, the reader should be reminded that at the automatic level the tests are not broken down into processes, but all four of the basic tests at this level are considered as whole-level tests. Comparisons of processes are, therefore, limited to comparing the averages of the two tests in each of the processes. Examples of these are given in a following section.

A *representational-level score* may be obtained with either scaled scores or age scores. It is obtained from the scores of the six basic tests at the representational level by dividing the sum of the scores by 6:

	Age Score	Scaled Score
Auditory Reception	4-10	28
Visual Reception	6-7	38
Auditory Association	4-9	22
Visual Association	7-7	42
Verbal Expression	5-2	30
Manual Expression	8-8	43
	34 years, 43 months	203
Mean	6-4	34

Similarly the *automatic-level score,* using either scaled scores or age scores, may be obtained by dividing the sum of the automatic-level scores by 4:

	Age Score	*Scaled Score*
Grammatic Closure	5-0	25
Visual Closure	6-6	37
Auditory Memory	4-2	27
Visual Memory	7-10	42
	22 years, 18 months	131
Mean	5-11	33

It will be noted that in John's case there appears to be little difference between the representational level (PLA, 6-4; SS, 34) and the automatic level (PLA, 5-11; SS, 33).

To obtain the *auditory-vocal channel score,* the sum of scores on the tests recorded in columns 1 and 3 of the Summary Sheet is divided by 5:

	Age Score	*Scaled Score*
Auditory Reception	4-10	28
Auditory Association	4-9	22
Verbal Expression	5-2	30
Grammatic Closure	5-0	25
Auditory Memory	4-2	27
	22 years, 23 months	132
Mean	4-9	26

To obtain the *visual-motor channel score,* the sum of the scores on the tests recorded in columns 2 and 4 (either age scores or scaled scores) is divided by 5:

	Age Score	*Scaled Score*
Visual Reception	6-7	38
Visual Association	7-7	42
Manual Expression	8-8	43
Visual Closure	6-6	37
Visual Memory	7-10	42
	34 years, 38 months	202
Mean	7-5	40

Figure

Profile of psycholinguistic a

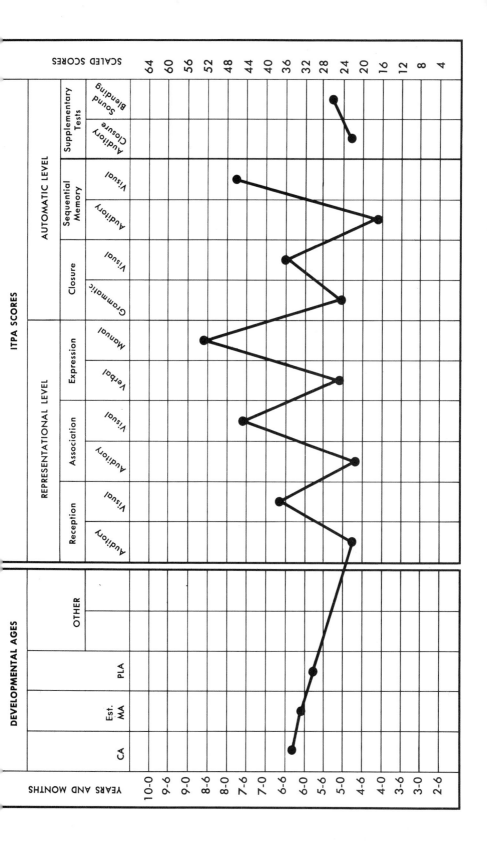

In John's case a comparison of the auditory-vocal with the visual-motor channel shows a discrepancy of two years, seven months, in age scores and 14 points in scaled scores.

In evaluating psycholinguistic processes, the scores for John appear as follows:

	PLA	PLQ	Scaled Score
Reception	5-9	92	33
Association	6-2	97	32
Expression	6-11	109	37

The differences in processes do not exceed ± 6 scaled scores; hence it is concluded that there is no significant difference in psycholinguistic processes.

The profile

The Record Form of the ITPA provides space for recording in graphic form the same scores shown on the Summary Sheet. Figure 5-2 is a profile of the psycholinguistic ages for each subtest, taken from Figure 5-1. This profile also presents on the left side such developmental age scores as CA, estimated MA, and PLA.

This form can be used for indicating either psycholinguistic ages (Figure 5-2) or scaled scores (Figure 5-3). If psycholinguistic ages are to be recorded, the scale at the left side of the page is used; if scaled scores are recorded, the scale on the right is used.

Looking at the Summary Sheet and the Profile of Abilities for the case of John as shown by Figures 5-1, 5-2, and 5-3, we must evaluate several aspects by inspecting the information presented.

The Profile of Abilities

Looking at the profile, some facts are immediately obvious. From the developmental information it can be seen that John was 6-4 at the time the ITPA was administered. His other developmental ages are not far from this but, looking at the profile of subtest scores, there are obvious discrepancies among the subtests. It is also obvious that the low points all occur in tests having to do with auditory or verbal tasks. We will return to this relationship later.

Global scores

Using John's CA of 6-4 as a reference point, one looks at the global scores obtained on the test: PLA, 5-10; PLQ, 92; mean

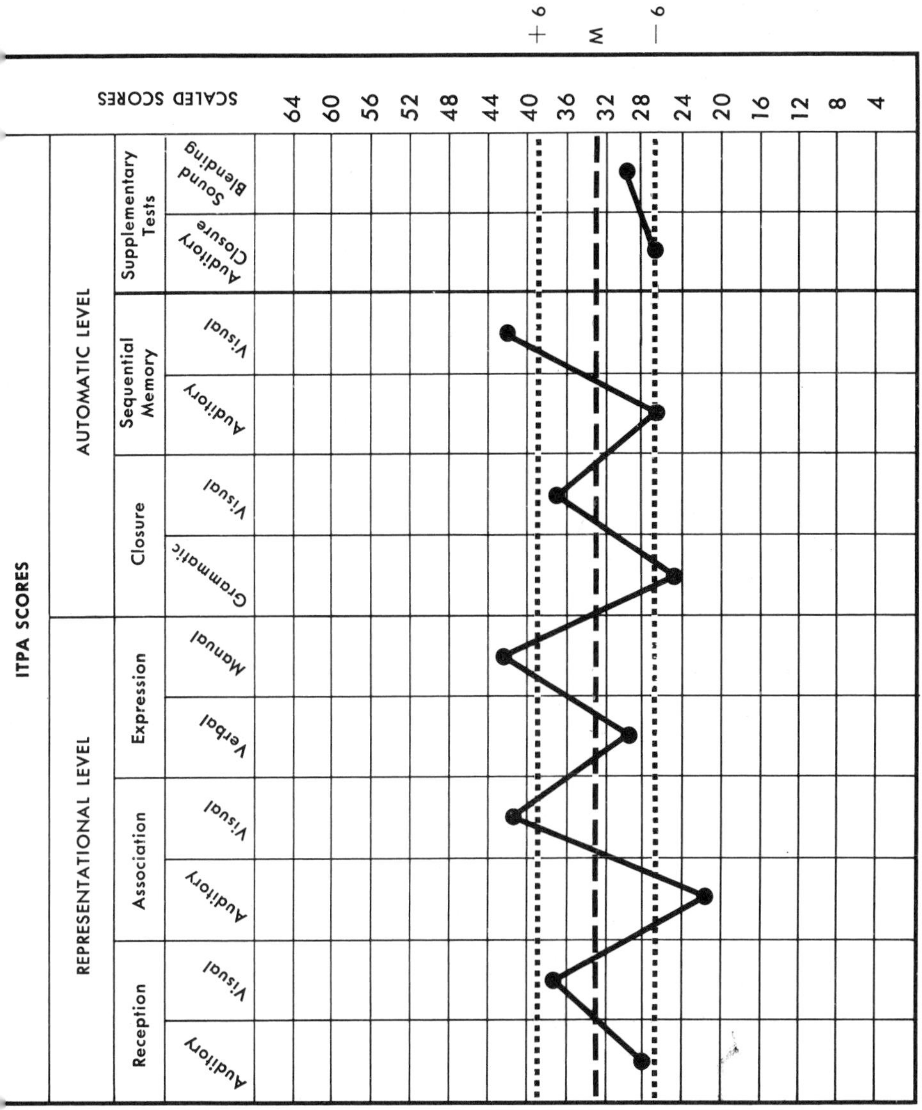

ITPA SCORES

SCALED SCORES

64 60 56 52 48 44 40 36 32 28 24 20 16 12 8 4

+6 M −6

REPRESENTATIONAL LEVEL

Reception
- Auditory
- Visual

Association
- Auditory
- Visual

Expression
- Verbal
- Manual

Closure
- Grammatic
- Visual

AUTOMATIC LEVEL

Sequential Memory
- Auditory
- Visual

Supplementary Tests
- Auditory Closure
- Sound Blending

Figure 5-3
Profile of scaled scores.

scaled score, 33.4; median scaled score, 33.5; estimated Stanford-Binet MA, 6-0; estimated Binet IQ, 94.

These scores suggest a child of average ability on global tests. His PLA and estimated MA of 5-10 and 6-0 are both within a few months of his CA; the PLQ of 92 and the estimated Binet IQ of 94 are both within the normal range; and the mean scaled score as well as the median scaled score are within a few points of the normative group average of 36.

Comparing part scores

Looking at the part scores derived for each of the three dimensions, we find the following:

	Age Score	*Quotient Score*	*Scaled Score*
Levels of organization			
Representational	6-4	100	34
Automatic	5-11	93	33
Channels of communication			
Auditory-vocal	4-9	75	26
Visual-motor	7-5	117	40
Psycholinguistic processes			
Reception	5-9	92	33
Association	6-2	97	32
Expression	6-11	109	37

It will be noted from the comparisons above that (a) there are no significant differences between the representational and automatic levels of organization, (b) there are no significant differences among the psycholinguistic processes, but (c) there is a significant difference between the visual-motor and auditory-vocal channels. In this case the auditory-vocal channel is two years, eight months, below and shows a scaled score 14 points below the visual-motor channel. This is the same area which was spotted by originally glancing at the profile, or "eyeballing" the profile, as some call it. Referring back to either of the profiles, it can be seen that this deficiency in the auditory-vocal channel is consistent; that is, all of the subtests in this area received low scores as compared to the visual-motor channel subtests.

The profile and the test scores also show marked superiority over the chronological age and over the PLA in Visual Association, Motor Expression, and Visual Sequential Memory, each of which is approximately two years above the PLA. All scores in this channel are above both the PLA and the CA. This is the kind of profile that is found in severely hard-of-hearing children and similar to profiles of children from foreign-language backgrounds. John, however, is not a member of either of these groups, which leads the examiner to believe that the child may have some idiosyncratic functional disability.

Comparing scores on separate functions

In looking at the deviation between scores, the question naturally arises as to how much of a deviation is meaningful. As stated in the *Examiner's Manual:*

1. Differences between a subtest SS and the mean or median SS of ±6 should not be considered an indication of a special ability or disability. This is the range within which over 80 percent of average children score.

2. Differences between the mean or median SS and a subtest SS of ±7, ±8, or ±9 are considered borderline discrepancies.

3. A difference between mean or median SS and a subtest SS of ±10 or greater is considered a substantial discrepancy; that is, a deviation of that magnitude is indicative of a discrepant function.

It should also be borne in mind that the pattern of deficiencies is very important. A deviation which might be considered only borderline on a single test takes on much more significance if it is consistent with a pattern of deficiencies. In the case of John, for instance, although all of the scaled scores in the auditory-vocal subtests are below the mean scaled score, only one of them (Auditory Association) is more than 9 scaled score points below. Furthermore, the scaled score of 26 on the auditory-vocal part score is only 7 points below the mean scaled score, but this does not mean that the deficiency is only borderline. The indication of a meaningful deficit is strengthened by the significance of the pattern of low scores all falling in the auditory-vocal channel.

To evaluate differences in performance among the various subtests, the examiner is directed to pp. 113 and 120 in *The Development and Psychometric Characteristics of the Revised Illinois Test of Psycholinguistic Abilities* (Paraskevopoulos and Kirk, 1969). The technique presented there evaluates the likelihood that the difference between two scores is statistically significant. Can one feel with any degree of certainty that the child really has a difference in ability in the two areas?

It must be borne in mind that no test score indicates with certainty the exact point at which a child is functioning. No individual functions exactly the same at all points in time, and no test is so exact that it measures identically each time. After all, a test is a sample of performance, and samples may differ. The more reliable a test, the more exact it may be in measuring the individual's ability.

The standard error of measurement (SE_m) of a test is an estimate of how much the test score, if given repeatedly, will vary from the "true" score. Similarly, the standard error of measurement of the difference (SE_{md}) between two test scores is an estimate of how much that difference may vary (within a reasonable probability) if the tests are repeated many times. The "true" score should be somewhere between X points above and X points below the score obtained on the test, assuming, of course, that the test has been administered according to the standardized procedure.

To illustrate this method of evaluating test score differences, we have compared all of John's low scores in the auditory-vocal channel with the lowest score in the visual-motor channel (Visual Closure) to see if these differences are "true" differences.

To compare SS differences, we turn to Table 7-9, p. 116, in *The Development and Psychometric Characteristics of the Revised ITPA* to find the standard error of measurement (SE_m) for each of the two tests we are comparing for a child of age 6-4. (Since data are not available for this particular age, the column of nearest ages is used. When the child's age is equidistant from two adjacent age groups, as in this case, the scores from the older group are utilized.) Using the SE_m found in Table 7-9 for the two tests, we find the letter designation for each from Table 7-10 and locate the intersection of these two in the table as explained in the directions. Using the data from Figure 5-1 and these two tables to find the SE_{md}, we find the following information in Table 5-1.

From Table 5-1 we find that in Auditory Reception John scored 9 SS points below Visual Closure (37-28) and that the standard error of measurement of the difference between these two scores is 4.1. In other words, the difference is at least two times the SE_{md} and this difference should be considered stable. Similarly, the difference between Visual Closure and Auditory Association is 15 SS points (37-22) and the SE_{md} is 4.5. This difference is three times

Table 5-1

ITPA Subtest	From Table 7-9[a]	From Table 7-10[b]		Scaled Score	Difference Score
	SE_m	Letter Interval	SE_{md}		
Visual Closure	3.6	M		37	
Auditory Reception	1.8	D	4.1	28	9**
Visual Closure	3.6	M		37	
Auditory Association	2.7	H	4.5	22	15***
Visual Closure	3.6	M		37	
Verbal Expression	3.0	J	4.8	30	7*
Visual Closure	3.6	M		37	
Grammatic Closure	3.2	K	4.9	25	12**
Visual Closure	3.6	M		37	
Auditory Memory	2.6	H	4.5	27	10**

[a] Paraskevopoulos and Kirk (1969), p. 116.
[b] *Ibid.*, pp. 118–119.

* = difference at least 1 SE_{md}.
** = difference at least 2 SE_{md}.
*** = difference at least 3 SE_{md}.

the SE_{md} and should be considered highly significant. The difference between Visual Closure and Verbal Expression is less marked (7 SS points) and it is between 1 and 2 SE_{md}. Thus we are still left with the confident conclusion that the auditory-vocal channel is John's weak area of functioning.

Summary

To recapitulate, there are several things to look for in viewing the test results on the ITPA.

1. In the first place, one looks at global scores to get a rough idea of the level of overall functioning the child displays. How do his scores compare with his chronological age and his school placement? How do they compare to the teacher's evaluation of the child? To the examiner's impression?

These global scores, like the individual scores, may be presented in terms of psycholinguistic ages or in the more statistically sophisticated form of scaled scores.

2. One also compares scores on individual subtests to note any atypical scores. Both the profile and Summary Sheet are helpful in seeing the relative level of ability indicated. The profile gives a

graphic representation of where the child stands in the various areas of ability; the statistical evaluation of the significance of different degrees of deviation helps decide whether a given deviation has a bearing on the child's disability.

3. The relationships among the tests and the patterns of abilities and disabilities are important in arriving at a hypothesis of why the child is failing and how he can best be helped. What confluence of related disabilities do we find? What is the interrelationship of these disabilities? Does an extremely low score in Auditory Sequential Memory explain why the child also has a low score in Verbal Expression, since he may not have been able to remember what he heard long enough to develop adequate ability to repeat what he heard and express his ideas in words and sentences? Has inability to express himself motorically affected his ability to see visual relationships?

The task still remains of devising a program through which John can best be helped to develop abilities in his weak area of functioning. Many other facets of behavior and development will have a bearing here. These will be discussed in later sections. It is very probable that in the case of John the program would emphasize oral communication and especially the development of auditory memory, auditory association, and grammatic and auditory closure. Verbal expression, although inferior to visual abilities, is not as defective as the other auditory functions and will automatically be dealt with in promoting the auditory abilities. Such remedial methods as the Bereiter-Engelmann approach, the Peabody Language Kits, and some aspects of the Johnson-Myklebust techniques would be appropriate here rather than the visual and perceptual training involved in the Frostig, Kephart, or Barsch approaches. John appears to be above average in functions involving visual and motor abilities, so the major emphasis should be on developing his auditory and verbal abilities.

Chapter six

Some
patterns
of
disabilities

Children's profiles differ widely in their indications of abilities and disabilities. Some children develop evenly in all areas while others have wide discrepancies among test scores, indicative of disabilities in some areas. Since there are so many ways in which these profiles vary, it is difficult to find any two profiles which are identical. Although disabilities may be classified in a number of ways, there are some general types of profiles which are commonly met. Figure 5-3 in Chapter 5 presents one common type of profile. This represents a child with an auditory-channel disability. An opposite profile in which the peaks and dips are reversed would indicate a child with a visual-channel disability. Some of the more common profiles would indicate the following deficits:

1. Channel deficits in which all (or most) of the subtests in the auditory-vocal channel or the visual-motor channel are below those in the other channel.

2. Channel deficits at only one level, e.g., if auditory and vocal tests at the representational level or at the automatic level are low.

3. Level deficits in which all of the functions at either the automatic level or the representational level are deficient.

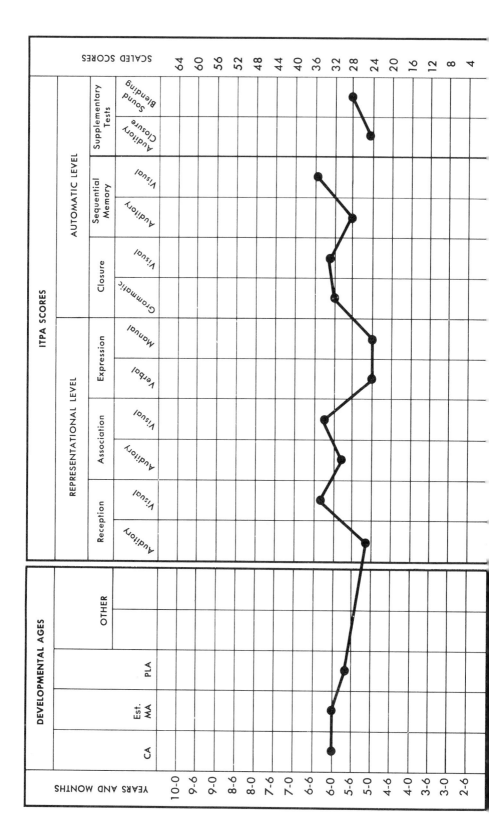

4. Process deficits in which the scores on subtests in one process are below the scores on other processes.

5. Other deficits, such as isolated deficits in one function or in two unrelated areas.

The following cases will illustrate some types of profiles. A brief commentary is provided for each case.

Profile for an average child

Figure 6-1 presents a profile of psycholinguistic ages for an average six-year-old child. It will be noted that the child's estimated Stanford-Binet mental age, as well as his CA, is 6-0, with an estimated IQ of 100. His composite PLA is 5-8 and none of the age scores for the subtests differs markedly from that level. The lowest PLA for any subtest is 5-0 on both verbal and manual expression; the highest is 6-6 in visual sequential memory. These deviations above or below the reference points (CA, MA, or composite PLA) are considered to be within the normal range. For this age child the discrepancy between the PLA and the subtests should be at least one and a half years before a disability is suspected.

Figure 6-2 presents the same test results in scaled scores. It will be noted from this profile that the mean scaled score is 35, quite consistent with the mean scaled score for an average child in the normative group. The scaled scores on the individual subtests for this child range from 31 to 38, none of which is more than 6 scaled score points (one standard deviation for the normative group) above or below his mean of 35. No special abilities or disabilities are indicated. According to these scaled scores, this child is considered developing evenly in all functions tested. In other words, these test results do not indicate any substantial intraindividual differences, and consequently remediation of psycholinguistic disabilities is not indicated.

Auditory-vocal channel disabilities

Figure 5-3, previously described in Chapter 5, presents the scores of a child with an auditory-vocal channel disability. There are, of course, numerous variations of this type of profile. Whereas Figure 5-3 presents a profile which shows considerable deficiency in all auditory and vocal functions as compared to the visual-motor channel functions, other children may show a channel disability only at

re 6-1

le of psycholinguistic ages for an average child.

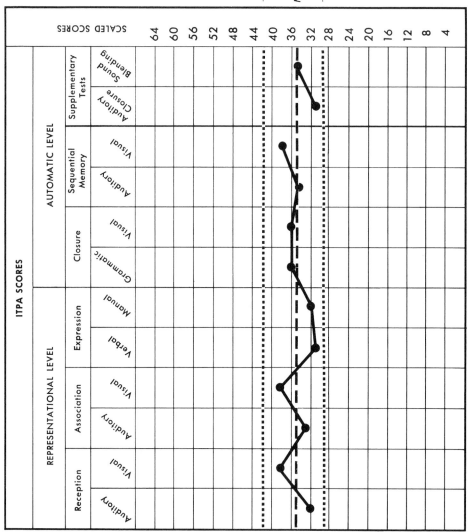

Figure 6-2

Profile of scaled scores for an average child.

the automatic level, while functions in the same channel at the representational level may not show marked deficits. A child could have adequate auditory reception, auditory association, and verbal expression, yet be deficient in grammatic closure, auditory sequential memory, auditory closure, and sound blending. The reverse may also occur, though it is less common.

Visual-motor channel disabilities

Visual-motor channel disabilities may be less common than auditory-vocal channel disabilities for school-age children, although, to the best of our knowledge, no such information has been scientifically determined. One possible explanation for this condition, if true, is that much of the seat work and workbooks in the primary grades stress visual-motor channel functions. The time the usual first-grade child spends on visual-motor channel exercises in workbooks is much greater than the time he spends in auditory-vocal interaction with the teacher. It should also be noted that although a child may be deprived of adequate verbal stimulation because of his social environment, visual stimuli are constantly impinging on his retina from his physical environment. Thus visual-motor channel deficits may be less frequent because the child is less often seriously deprived of visual experience.

Figure 6-3 presents the profile for a child who is five years, eleven months, of age. His composite PLA is 5-9 and his estimated Stanford-Binet MA is 5-11. His profile shows marked discrepancies in psycholinguistic ages with PLAs of 3-4 in manual expression and 8-7 in auditory sequential memory, a discrepancy of approximately five years. Both verbal expression and auditory sequential memory, with PLAs of 8-4 and 8-7 respectively, show abilities more than two and a half years above the composite PLA of 5-9. The major disabilities are in visual association (4-6), manual expression (3-4), visual closure (4-0), and visual sequential memory (4-4). These functions appear to be one and a half years or more below the composite PLA. Visual reception is below auditory reception, but the discrepancy is less than one year, which is not considered significant.

To determine whether these abilities are significantly deficient, scaled scores are used as presented in Figure 6-4. This profile shows a mean scaled score of 35. Using the criterion of ±6 scaled score points as indicating a possible disability, we find that visual reception (SS, 33) is within the average range, but that visual

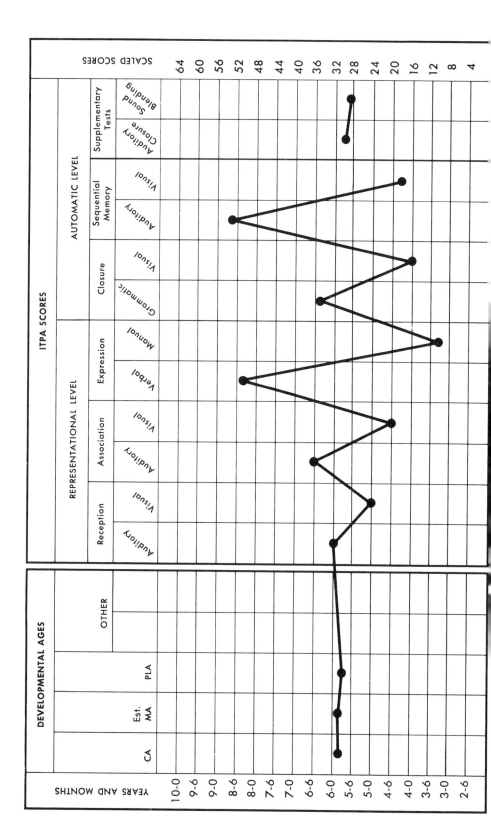

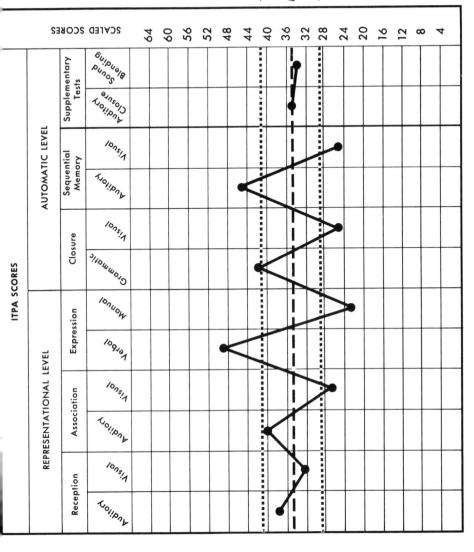

Figure 6-4

Profile of scaled scores for a child with a visual-channel disability.

Figure 6-3

Profile of psycholinguistic ages for a child with a visual-channel disability.

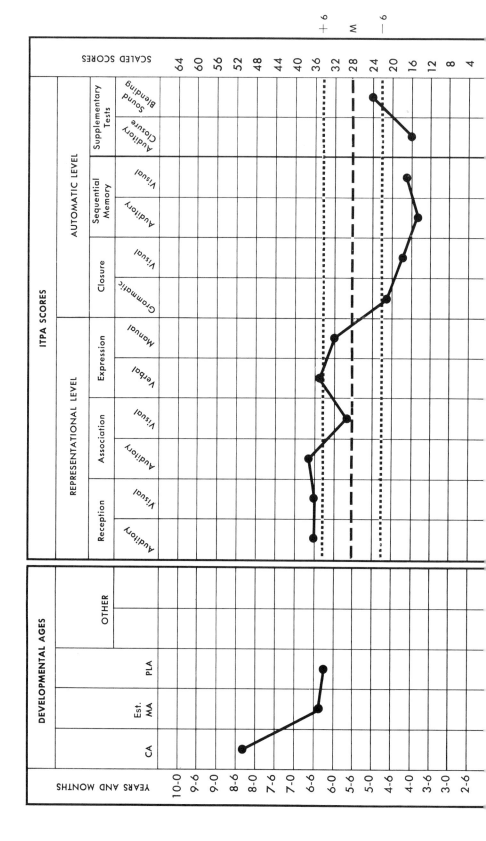

association (SS, 27), manual expression (SS, 23), visual closure (SS, 25), and visual sequential memory (SS, 25) are all more than 6 scaled score points below the mean scaled score. Although not all of the visual and motor tests are significantly low, they are all below their auditory counterparts. It would appear that this child is definitely deficient in visual-motor channel functions and that a program of training to ameliorate this channel deficiency is needed. Chapter 9 describes briefly some guidelines for remediation of visual-motor deficits.

A level disability

Figure 6-5 presents the profile of scaled scores for a child aged 8-4. His composite PLA is 6-3, with a PLQ of 75. His mean scaled score is 28, indicating subnormal overall development in psycholinguistic abilities. A perusal of the profile in Figure 6-5 shows that this child is relatively average on most of the tests at the representational level. The six tests of the representational level range from a scaled score of 29 on visual association to 37 on auditory association with a mean scaled score of 34 at the representational level. On all tests at the automatic level he performs below a scaled score of 22 (from a low scaled score of 15 in auditory sequential memory to a scaled score of 21 for grammatic closure). The mean scaled score for the four basic tests at the automatic level is 18, 10 points below his mean scaled score of 28 for the whole test and 16 scaled score points below the average scaled score of 34 for the representational level. The basic disabilities are in auditory and visual closure and in auditory and visual sequential memory. Although this child functions normally in school in oral discussions and interpersonal activities, he is retarded in reading, writing, and spelling. A remedial program in reading and spelling should extract from his reading materials exercises to develop auditory closure and sequential memory in relation to the remedial reading and spelling program. It is very common for mentally retarded children to have low scores on subtests at the automatic level and relatively higher scores at the representational level. This raises some doubt as to training goals for the mentally retarded. Have we been overemphasizing meaningful material at the expense of the development of certain fundamental, automatic abilities and skills which might in

ͼure 6-5

ɔfile of scaled scores for a child
:h an automatic-level disability.

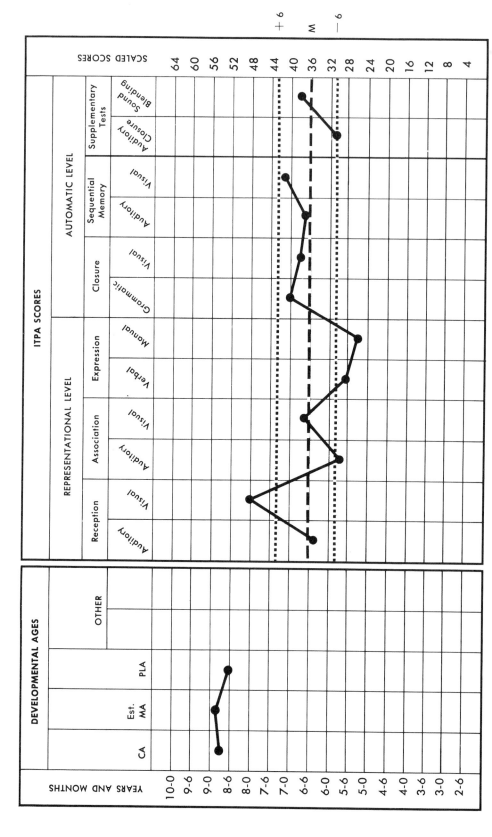

the long run make understanding of meaningful material easier? Should we provide more of the redundancies which develop automatic responses before or during the development of symbolic processes at the representational level?

Process disabilities

Disabilities may occur in any of the three processes or in various combinations. A few examples may suffice to illustrate typical process disabilities.

Expressive disabilities

Figure 6-6 presents the scaled scores of a boy of 8-9. His composite PLA is 8-6 and his PLQ is 96. The mean scaled score is 36. These global scores classify this boy as of average ability. A perusal of the profile, however, indicates a superiority in visual reception but significant disabilities in verbal expression (SS, 28) and manual expression (SS, 22) and possibly in auditory association (SS, 30). These scaled scores deviate from his mean SS of 36 by -8, -10, and -6 respectively. This boy's remedial program to reduce the deficits in expression would concentrate on meaningful expressive exercises, both verbal and motor. See Figure 3-2 for the profile of a child with a marked expressive disability who responded to remediation.

A more common type of expressive disability is found in children who have a wide discrepancy between verbal and manual expression. Figure 6-7 shows a child of six years of age who has a marked discrepancy between his manual expressive ability (PLA, 9-10; SS, 46) and his verbal expressive ability (PLA, 5-0; SS, 30). In this case the child is also low in auditory sequential memory (PLA, 3-9; SS, 27) and grammatic closure (PLA, 4-8; SS, 23). His profile suggests an auditory-vocal channel disability, but the major deficiencies are in the psycholinguistic functions noted. One can hypothesize from this profile that the deficiency in auditory sequential memory during the growing stages has inhibited his ability to acquire verbal fluency, since he probably could not "keep in mind" the total sentences he heard in his natural environment. This deficiency may also have contributed to his inabil-

re **6-6**

le of scaled scores for a child
an expressive disability.

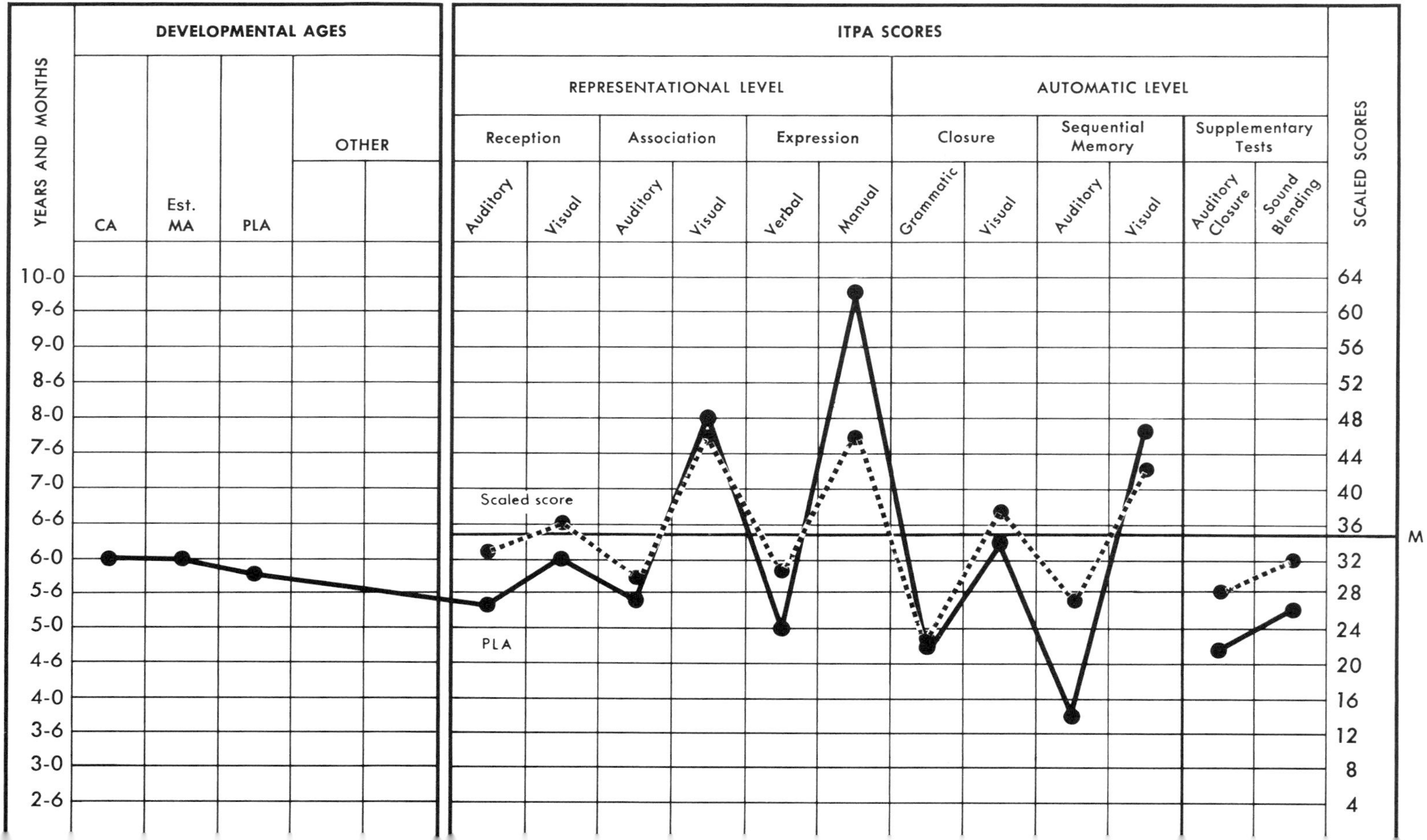

	DEVELOPMENTAL AGES				ITPA SCORES											
YEARS AND MONTHS				OTHER	REPRESENTATIONAL LEVEL						AUTOMATIC LEVEL						SCALED SCORES
					Reception		Association		Expression		Closure		Sequential Memory		Supplementary Tests		
	CA	Est. MA	PLA		Auditory	Visual	Auditory	Visual	Verbal	Manual	Grammatic	Visual	Auditory	Visual	Auditory Closure	Sound Blending	

Scale (left, Years and Months): 10-0, 9-6, 9-0, 8-6, 8-0, 7-6, 7-0, 6-6, 6-0, 5-6, 5-0, 4-6, 4-0, 3-6, 3-0, 2-6

Scale (right, Scaled Scores): 64, 60, 56, 52, 48, 44, 40, 36 (M), 32, 28, 24, 20, 16, 12, 8, 4

Labels within chart: Scaled score; PLA

ity to acquire grammatic closure. The remedial program should organize activities that would train verbal abilities, with sufficient redundancies to aid grammatic closure and with emphasis on the development of auditory sequential memory in relation to the training of verbal expression.

Association disabilities

One can find an auditory association disability with a visual association superiority and vice versa, or one can find a disability in both association functions. Figure 6-8 presents the profile of a child who has disabilities in both auditory and visual association. In this case the child is six years, eight months, of age. His composite PLA is 5-0, estimated MA is 5-4, with an estimated IQ of 78. The mean scaled score is 26, 10 points below that of an average child; and on all subtests this child fell below a scaled score of 36. This would suggest that the child is of below-average ability, as is also indicated by a PLQ of 75 and an estimated Binet IQ of 78. This boy had been tested on the Stanford-Binet several times. Because of delay in speech, he had been tested at the age of five. At that time he obtained an IQ of 75 on the Stanford-Binet. When he was six the Stanford-Binet was again administered, resulting in an IQ of 78.

The only noteworthy deviation in scores in this profile occurs in auditory and visual association. On these two subtests the boy scored 11 and 9 points respectively below his mean scaled score, indicating that he has difficulty in the association process. He does not grasp relationships and probably has difficulty holding two concepts in mind and seeing them in juxtaposition.

The emphasis in the remedial program for this child would consist of exercises, games, and activities that are focused on the amelioration of the association deficit. To organize such a program, it is necessary to observe the school environment in which he is placed and to alter the program so that emphasis will be given to the deficit. A discussion of guidelines for the development of remedial programs for association abilities is found in Chapter 9.

Reception disabilities

Rarely will one find severe disabilities in both auditory and visual

ɔfile of scaled scores and PLAs for a child
ſh a verbal expressive disability.

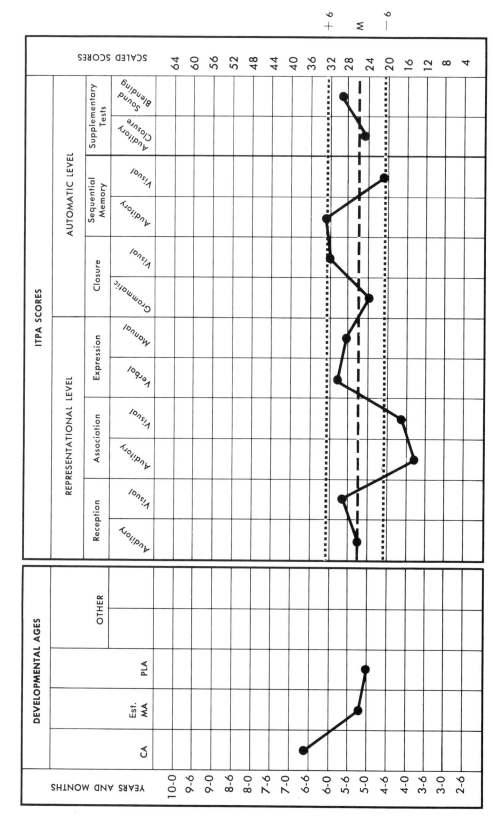

reception with superior abilities in auditory and visual association and expression. If input in these sense modalities is severely blocked (over a two-year discrepancy), the association and expressive processes have difficulties in developing. The deaf-blind child, using an extreme case, substitutes the haptic modality for visual input and the associations that are developed are the result of haptic inputs.

Mentally retarded children

It has been found that the classification of children as mentally retarded on the basis of IQ results in a heterogeneous group of children. Children with the same IQ may have different abilities and disabilities.

Figure 6-9 shows the profile of scaled scores for a child classified as mentally retarded. He is five years, eight months, of age, and on a previous Stanford-Binet examination he obtained an IQ of 77. On the ITPA he obtained a PLA of 4-6 and an estimated Stanford-Binet MA of 4-7. His estimated Binet IQ was 79. His profile of psycholinguistic abilities shows that he has no scores more than 6 points above or below his mean scaled score of 28. It is inferred that he is equally retarded in all psycholinguistic abilities.

Figure 6-10 shows the scaled score profile of another boy, six years, seven months, of age, who had obtained a Stanford-Binet IQ of 71. On the ITPA he obtained a composite PLA of 4-11, a mean scaled score of 28, an estimated Stanford-Binet MA of 5-0, and an estimated Binet IQ of 73. This profile of scaled scores shows a different picture from the immediately preceding profile in spite of the similarities in global scores. In this case the child has average or near-average abilities in visual reception, visual association, manual expression, visual closure, and visual sequential memory. His scaled

re **6-8**

le of scaled scores for a child
an association disability.

Figure 6-9

Profile of scaled scores for a mentally retarded child with no substantial abilities or disabilities.

Figure 6-10

Profile of scaled scores for a child mistakenly classified as mentally retarded.

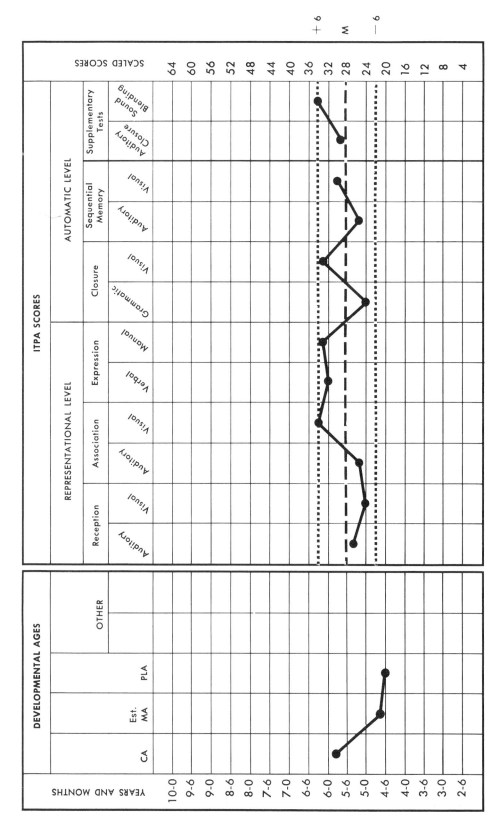

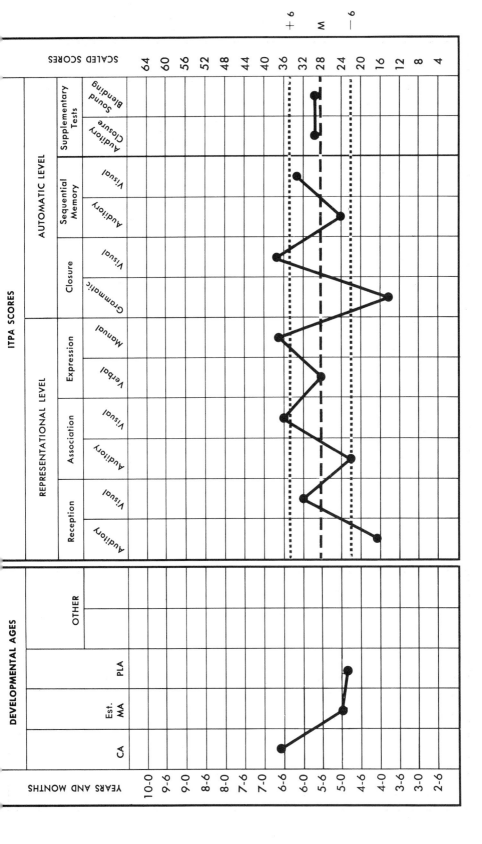

scores on visual-motor functions averaged 35, but his scaled scores on the auditory-vocal tests averaged only 21. He appears to have definite disabilities in auditory reception and grammatic closure, with probably a generalized disability in the auditory-vocal channel relative to his abilities in the visual-motor channel. This child comes from an Indian family, and although he has been in integrated schools, his home and community environment did not provide him with English language patterns. Such a child should not be classified as mentally retarded but, rather, as a child with a learning disability. The remedial program should emphasize auditory and oral language experiences.

Other deficits

In addition to the more common deficits described in the preceding sections, there will be found many less typical combinations of deficits in children. Occasionally there will be a deficit in only one area or there may be depressed functions in apparently unrelated areas. For example, children may have high visual reception and low auditory reception but adequate auditory association and low visual association. In such cases the child's abilities are blocked in both channels. In one channel he is blocked at intake and in the other channel he can receive information but cannot manipulate the concepts he receives.

The examiner should be cautioned not to accept discrepancies in profiles that do not conform to a rational diagnosis without checking with observations and other tests. For example, one examiner found a child who scored at the 3-2 age level in auditory reception and 7-5 in auditory association. In grammatic closure the child scored at the 4-0 age level. The question here is, how can a child score four years above his other auditory tests in auditory association if he has a significant deficit in auditory reception? A check of the test blank explained the discrepancy. An arithmetic error had been made and, when corrected, the child's PLA on auditory association was 5-7.

Another example may be cited. A child, age 8-5, in the third grade was still a nonreader. On the ITPA he obtained an estimated Binet IQ of at least 126 since he scored above the norms on some of the tests. His profile showed no significant deficits in psycholinguistic abilities which could explain his severe reading disability. Tests of orientation showed a child who had marked reversal errors but who was distinctly right-handed. His basic inhibitions to learning were found in the motor perceptual area rather than in psycho-linguistic deficits as assessed by the ITPA.

Chapter 7 is devoted to suggestions for supplementary diagnosis and classroom observations. These are included to assist the diagnostician in checking the disabilities found on the ITPA and for further assessing the extent and range of the disability.

Suggestions for further analysis and diagnosis

The full assessment of children's abilities and disabilities requires a progressive type of diagnosis. The use of omnibus tests like the Stanford-Binet Intelligence Scale (Terman and Merrill, 1960) or the Wechsler Intelligence Scale for Children (WISC) (Wechsler, 1949) is considered an initial step for the purpose of classifying a child as high, average, or low in general cognitive abilities. A second stage in diagnosis is the use of tests of specific intellectual, perceptual, and/or cognitive factors. The twelve subtests of the ITPA were designed to locate discrepancies among abilities and disabilities of the child. As indicated earlier, such a diagnosis, supported and investigated further by other tests and observations, should lead to a remedial program.

Limitations of the ITPA

Before discussing diagnostic procedure in detail, it must be pointed out that the ITPA, like all tests, has limitations. These limitations are noted below.

1. The ITPA is applicable to children whose mental levels are between two and a half and nine and a half years of age. It is not applicable to children over the CA of ten.

2. Although the norms of the ITPA go down as low as two years, it should be emphasized that at this age level caution must be used in interpreting scores. Children whose mental ages are below three years cannot show a very definitive profile of disabilities since no score can go below two years. Any deficit below that would be obscured by the lower limits of the test. It should also be remembered that because of extraneous factors, it is very difficult to obtain a reliable test score on two-year-old children.

3. Scores at the nine- to ten-year level are also questionable since success on one item more or less may change the age score by several months, and on many of the subtests the scaled scores do not provide a high enough ceiling at these ages. Scores above age levels of eight and a half should be interpreted with caution. The test is not suitable for children with mental levels much above eight and a half or nine years except to determine special areas of deficit. The limitations imposed by the ceilings of many of the subtests obscure higher abilities.

4. The ITPA does not assess all abilities and disabilities. Other abilities and disabilities often can be suspected from the shape of the profile which, together with clinical observations, may suggest supplementary or additional tests to be given. A case in point is the suspicion of poor body image from a low score on manual expression.

5. The ITPA does not circumvent the effects of cultural factors. Every examiner must be cognizant of these effects on test results. A child from a language-deprived home, for example, could understandably be deficient on the Grammatic Closure subtest of the ITPA, since this subtest involves grammatical usage to which he may not be accustomed. Although an effort has been made to eliminate from this test items frequently misused by adults using nonstandard English, some of these do remain and should be noted in evaluating a child's score. Analysis of the items failed in some cases may mitigate a low score as indicating a disability in auditory closure or the ability to acquire automatic responses. It would indicate, instead, that certain auditory experiences would pass this child by because of his deficient background, and this omission could affect the development of other functions.

6. A child who is flighty and hard to interest in the tasks or a

child who has a generalized anxiety may show an exaggeration of his deficits or may cause some tests to be invalidated by extraneous factors. His weakest areas, which he tends to avoid, might conceivably be affected most, which in itself might be of added significance diagnostically.

7. Variable rapport, examiner bias, and anxiety or lack of cooperation on the part of the child may cause a distortion of the profile. One should always remember that the mechanical use of tests can lead to faulty diagnosis when isolated from clinical judgment and indications from other data. For these reasons, supplementary tests, observations, and diagnoses are necessary when there is any question or doubt, especially when the information obtained from the ITPA is not consistent with other tests or with observations.

A more complete model
of the communication process

A more complete model of the communication process is presented in Figure 7-1. It is termed a clinical model to emphasize the relationship to observable behavior rather than to theoretical background. It comprises a frame of reference or guideline for determining not only what areas of known or suspected disability should be examined further but also how such further diagnosis can be related to the obtained ITPA profile.

Like the ITPA model described earlier, this model includes channels of communication, levels of organization, and psycholinguistic processes. This expanded model clarifies certain relationships and includes functions not directly tapped by the ITPA. Among these functions are:

1. *The haptic (tactile plus kinesthetic) input channel or sense modality.* Haptic input plays a much more important role in the education of blind children (e.g., learning Braille) and deaf children (certain motor-kinesthetic techniques for developing speech) than it does with children whose auditory and visual channels are intact, but its use in general education is often ignored where it could be utilized as an adjunct to other receptive processes.

2. *Nonsymbolic reception* (the discrimination or discernment of auditory, visual, and haptic stimuli at the automatic level). Developing these functions is prerequisite to successful reception at

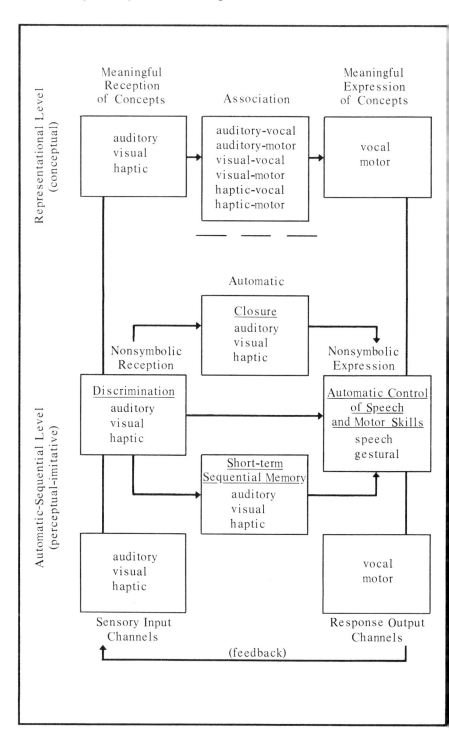

the meaningful level as well as to success in remembering and repeating what has been experienced at the automatic level. If a child shows difficulty with auditory or visual reception at the representational level, his ability to perceive and discern visual and auditory stimuli should be checked. For example, a deaf child who has difficulty with lip reading (conceptual visual reception) may need to first overcome a deficit in visual discrimination ability. Likewise, a child cannot be expected to remember a series of digits that he has not adequately heard and discriminated.

3. *Visual-vocal, auditory-motor, haptic-vocal, and haptic-motor association abilities.* Within the organizing process channels may be freely crossed in actual communication. Information obtained strictly by visual input, for example, can later be employed in vocal expression. Full crossing of input and output modes in the association process illustrates this transfer and interrelating of information from various sense modalities.

4. *Haptic sequential memory.* This model adds haptic sequential memory (or the ability to remember and repeat a sequence of movements or haptic experiences) to the auditory and visual sequential memory included in the ITPA.

5. *Nonsymbolic expression.* This ability, not tapped by the ITPA, involves the capacity to perform those routine acts of speech and movement which make communication possible. During the infant's stage of babbling, he produces many more sounds than any one language uses. Through contact with his environment and the hearing of certain sounds and not others, he tends to drop out of his repertoire those sounds and combinations of sounds he does not hear. These particular redundancies vary from culture to culture; thus the Japanese child finds it difficult to use our "r" sound and the American child finds it difficult to use the French "u" or certain combinations such as "mb" in Mboya or "nk" in Nkruma or Russian words like "vsaw" or "gde."

This level of expressive ability includes the central nervous system's control of these speech and motor skills so that the individual can put them into action on demand.

ıre 7-1

ical model of the communication process.

Supplementary diagnosis

As indicated earlier, the twelve subtests of the ITPA make possible an assessment of ten psycholinguistic functions, even though there are more functions, as shown in Figure 7-1, that can be isolated. The following are some supplementary observations and tests that can be used not only to confirm or reject a diagnosis based on the twelve subtests but also to supplement the diagnosis with those details which need to be isolated if an adequate remedial program is to be devised.

An example of what is meant by a supplementary diagnosis follows. Figure 5-3 shows the profile of a child who is very low in auditory reception and who also shows deficits in other auditory-vocal abilities. The expanded communication model shown in Figure 7-1 indicates that the ability to recognize and discriminate auditory stimuli is basic to meaningful auditory reception. The diagnostician will want to check auditory discrimination either informally or by such a test as Wepman's (1958) Auditory Discrimination Test. If auditory discrimination is adequate, then one has more confidence in organizing a remedial program specifically for meaningful understanding of verbal stimuli. If auditory discrimination is defective, however, the diagnostician will want to trace the difficulty still further and have auditory acuity examined by an audiologist to determine whether the difficulty is peripheral or central. If auditory acuity is adequate and is not the basis of the difficulty, remedial instruction should begin with exercises in auditory training and discrimination and later progress to auditory reception.

The following suggestions are given for supplementary diagnosis for different disabilities found on the ITPA. The specific tests or observational techniques suggested are illustrative only and not exhaustive.

The diagnostician must note carefully the age level at which the disability in question appears to exist and make comparisons with other evidence at a comparable level of functioning. For example, if a nine-year-old child receives a psycholinguistic age score of 5-6 on the ITPA Auditory Association test, we would expect that he would pass the Binet opposite analogies at years four and four and a half, but fail at years six and seven. Were he to pass opposite analogies on the Binet at a level higher than six years, some doubt would be cast on the validity of either the ITPA or the Binet score.

In the case of severe disabilities many ITPA subtest scores can be checked by observing the child's behavior in nontesting situations. For example, the child with a deficit on the Manual Expression test might show a noticeable developmental lag in self-help and motor activities, such as dressing or in dramatics. An unusually severe case of a visual reception deficit which has been brought to our attention was one in which the youngster was literally unable to recognize members of his own class by visual means, although his visual acuity was normal according to assessments by three ophthalmologists. He identified children by recognizing their voices.

Auditory reception

If a child has a marked deficit in auditory reception, it is probable that other tests or teacher observations would confirm the results of the ITPA. The diagnostician will want to note indications of auditory reception difficulty from such other tests as the Peabody Picture Vocabulary Test (PPVT) (Dunn, 1965). It should be borne in mind that the results of this test are ambiguous in that it requires receptive ability in two sense modalities, the auditory and the visual. A low score on the PPVT may be affected by poor receptive ability in either channel. However, if the child is high on visual reception on the ITPA and is low on auditory reception, one would suspect that his low score on the PPVT resulted from difficulty in auditory reception.

Similarly, many test items on the Binet, although contaminated by visual reception, verbal expression, and other requirements, do emphasize auditory reception. Identification of parts of the body, identification of objects by name, identification of objects by use, and pictorial identification require such a low level of visual reception or of verbal or manual expression that failure on these items indicates poor auditory reception. Comprehension and following commands on the Binet, as well as some of the verbal instructions and such concepts as "same" and "different," also require auditory receptive abilities. The WISC verbal should also be examined.

If it is decided that auditory reception is a major deficiency, the examiner should attempt to track the difficulty to a lower level to see if a deficiency in auditory discrimination is present. This may be tested informally by asking the child to tell if a pair of words (e.g., "hit, hip"; "see, she"; "lift, left") sound the same or different. A more objective measure of this ability may be obtained by use of standardized tests of auditory discrimination. If the child fails to note such differences, one should investigate the possibility of a sensory difficulty and obtain a test of auditory acuity.

Any environmental factors which may have contributed to difficulty in comprehending the spoken word (such as early hearing loss, bilingualism in the home, or hearing or linguistic deficits in other members of the family) should also be noted.

In observing classroom behavior a teacher may observe a child who seems to be normally intelligent in other areas but who is unable to grasp more than very simple short directions. The teacher may have to repeat individually directions to such a child. Or she may have to demonstrate what she wants or get him started individually. He usually understands directions or stories better if pictures or diagrams or even gestures are used. He is the child who needs visual aids and dramatic gestures to supplement verbal information. He may need to be led or otherwise physically directed when told to sit down or turn around. In extreme cases the teacher often suspects a hearing loss and refers the child for an audiometric examination. Sometimes the teacher says, "He just won't listen," or "He doesn't try to understand," or "He is just daydreaming," or "He's just ornery." It seems impossible that he can't understand plain English. Sometimes these children do not respond well to other children. They don't understand what other childern are talking about. They may feel left out or get their feelings hurt. On the other hand, they may do well in active games or take the lead so that they do not have to depend so much on the auditory receptive factor. Or they may be unusually cognizant of gestures and subtle expressions. They often want to work alone rather than in a group or on a team.

They do not enjoy stories and prefer television to the radio. They usually avoid word games, and in games which require a response to verbal directions they usually follow what they see the other children doing rather than respond to the verbal directions. They appear slow to respond. Their passive vocabulary is low and is sometimes reflected in a low active vocabulary. They may be able to repeat what they hear even though they do not understand it. Sometimes repeating it out loud helps them to interpret what they hear, as does repeating it to them slowly.

Visual reception

In evaluating a child's low score on the Visual Reception test, the diagnostician would look for other indications of poor performance on tasks requiring understanding of visually presented material.

A poor score on the Peabody Picture Vocabulary Test in the face of success on tests of auditory reception might indicate poor visual reception. The diagnostician might examine the child's responses on the Binet tests of picture vocabulary, aesthetic comparison, and picture absurdities. Response to pictures (at III-6 and VI), although contaminated with other requirements, also involves visual reception, as do many of the performance subtests of the WISC.

Tests for further diagnosis should include tests of more basic visual perception or discrimination. If a child cannot make simple discriminations of a nonsymbolic nature, he will be unable to gain meaning from symbolic visual stimuli. Such tests might include the tests of perceptual speed in the SRA Primary Mental Abilities Test (Thurstone and Thurstone, 1953), the form discrimination tests from the Minnesota Preschool Scale (Goodenough, Maurer, and Van Wagenen, 1940), and the Binet. Pictorial similarities and differences at years IV-6 and V on the Binet are also tests of visual discrimination. At a lower level, failure on the comparison of balls, comparison of sticks, and discrimination of animals might indicate difficulty in this area. Parts of the Columbia Mental Maturity Scale (Burgemeister, Blum, and Lorge, 1954) are appropriate in this category for young children.

In examining difficulties in visual perception, Frostig's (1964) Developmental Tests of Visual Perception are helpful in further delineating specific types of difficulty. This test includes measures of eye-hand coordination, figure-ground perception, form constancy, position in space, and spatial relationships. The norms range from about three to ten years of age.

The Developmental Form Sequence Test (Beery and Buktenica, 1967) appears very fruitful for the study of visual form perception, organization, and reproduction. Approximate age levels can be assigned to every form attempted, and an overall age equivalent is available based on norms for ages from about two to fourteen years for both sexes. This test involves more than visual perception, for manual expression is also involved and probably some organizing functions and motor skills at the automatic level.

A child showing difficulties in visual perception should, of course, be further examined for possible sensory defects in the visual field. Not only should refractive errors be determined but any problems of fusion, muscle imbalance, depth perception, etc. should be evaluated and corrected when possible.

Informally, it will frequently be observed that the child with poor visual reception ability has not cared much for picture books and is slow in identifying pictures of objects. He fails to get context clues reading from the illustrations in readers and frequently cannot explain what is happening. When asked to rearrange a series of pictures in their proper order, he may have difficulty. Often he can succeed better if he is asked to verbalize what is happening in each picture.

He is often slow in completing his workbook assignments and frequently has to have the teacher tell him verbally what is expected. He responds better to spoken words than to visual aids, and often the use of such gestures as pointing, "go away," or "come here" do not get the expected results. He is sometimes insensitive to grimaces and facial expressions.

Auditory association

The Auditory Association subtest has been described as assessing "the ability to draw relationships from what is heard" or as "the ability to manipulate linguistic symbols internally" (Kirk and McCarthy, 1961, p. 403). The completion of any analogy requires that the subject manipulate concepts internally in such a way as to find meaningful relationships. It is necessary for the child to hold two concepts in mind and find their parallel aspects—to understand not only the two isolated concepts but the relationship between them. A drawer, for example, holds the same relationship to a desk as a pocket does to a pair of trousers; the hammer a carpenter uses corresponds to the paintbrush a painter uses.

In seeking confirmation or denial of the results of this subtest, one might examine the child's ability on the opposite analogies subtest of the Binet at years II, VI, and VII in relation to his general level of ability. Also, tests of similarities and differences, opposite analogies, and verbal absurdities might give some clue as to the child's ability to see logical relationships. The similarities subtest of the WISC and other similar tests may also be given.

Children who function inadequately in this area often have difficulty categorizing objects verbally, as in the game of Beast, Bird, or Fish. They seldom use similes and metaphors. It is difficult for them to grasp the idea of sets and subsets or outlining material. They are slow to respond to tasks requiring generalizations. They have difficulty relating the moral of a story because it is difficult for them to see the correspondence between the abstract situation and the tangible example given in the story. They may not detect incongruities in absurd statements. They may have trouble solving riddles or understanding puns, proverbs, and parables. They may also fail to understand a joke or see what is funny in verbal absurdities. They do not see relationships like whole-part, tool-user, opposites, size, temperature, or texture. Frequently they have difficulty saying in what way things are alike or different.

Children with this difficulty often do foolish things because they do not see the present situation in relationship to past experience or future consequences. They do not see the two situations in juxtaposition. It is often difficult for them to generalize from one situation to another. In the story of Epaminandes the little boy did not have this ability and when his mother told him to lead the puppy home with a piece of string, he did not see how dragging home a loaf of bread with a piece of string was different.

If difficulty is suspected in auditory association and is confirmed by examination of related test items and other behavior, the diagnostician should look at such other auditory-channel functions as auditory memory and auditory reception. However, it has been found that an association deficit can exist in relative isolation.

Visual association

Visual association is the organizing process whereby a child sees the relationships between concepts presented visually. Here again the child must keep the two concepts in mind and recognize the point-to-point correspondence between them. The requisite here seems to be a second order of comprehension derived from visual impressions. In a first order of comprehension, a child may comprehend a picture of a hammer and a picture of a carpenter but not recognize the second-order relationship of tool and user. He must see that a pin and a thimble have a relationship to each other in that they are used together in sewing.

Tests to further check on whether a visual association disability exists could include the Raven Progressive Matrices (1947) or the Healy Picture Completion Tests, I and II. There are many tests of visual association included in such tests as the Columbia Mental Maturity Scale (1954), Minnesota Preschool Scale (1940), the Leiter International Scale (1955), and others. Reading readiness materials that include drawing a line from a word to a correct choice among a group of pictures, although contaminated with reading ability, are also related. The process of classification of pictures by putting all things to wear into one pile and to eat in another would determine if the child could recognize and separate elements according to function.

When asked to tell about a picture, a child with poor visual association is more apt to describe objects or label them than to tell a story or relate various parts of the picture. He may also do poorly in craft work because he does not see the relationships among materials or develop parallel ideas to other things he has seen.

These children often fail to see absurdities in pictures and have difficulty grasping the content of a story from a series of pictures. They may have difficulty putting a series of pictures in the right sequence because they do not understand the temporal relationships. They may fail to use context clues from the illustrations, although it is often difficult to know without other information whether this is due to a difficulty in visual association or visual reception.

Verbal expression

Verbal expression is the ability to put one's ideas into words. As measured by the ITPA, it involves the *intent* to express a concept as well as the actual verbal ability. It takes into account the number of discrete, relevant, and factual ideas the child can express but does not reflect the elegance of expression or grammatical propriety.

Evidence of a vocal expression disability may also be found from responses to other tests. The Binet tests of vocabulary, verbal response to pictures, definitions, picture absurdities, and the tests of vocabulary on the WISC may all suggest a verbal expression disability. Some projective tests and informal observation give the examiner many opportunities to recognize the child's ability to express himself verbally. His ability here should, of course, be viewed in relation to mental age, personality, and family background. The examiner should be familiar with levels of normal language development.

Emotional inhibition and family habits of reticence may also affect responses on this test, but the diagnostician should sparingly discount a low score on the basis of personality unless there are definite indications that the child can and does express himself in other situations. It has been our experience that reticence on this test is most often due to poor expressive ability rather than poor expressive ability being due to reticence.

Sometimes a thorough speech analysis may be indicated when a verbal expression disability is present. Severe articulation disorders and/or other speech problems can be underlying factors of poor or limited verbal expression ability. Speech training, of course, should be undertaken where disabilities in articulation or other speech problems inhibit growth in verbal expression. But it should be recognized that often the rest of the speech problem lies in the perceptual and cognitive difficulties which make it hard for the child to express ideas. His inability to predict and use customary habits of speech, for example, could be the basis for both poor articulation and poor verbal expression, rather than poor articulation causing poor verbal expression.

It is important, therefore, that the examiner evaluate other correlates of poor verbal expression. Does the child lack the basic vocal skills which make speech flow freely? Does he lack the content of ideas to express? Does he have an adequate receptive and/or expressive vocabulary? Is he able to organize his ideas and delimit the relevant from the irrelevant? It is necessary to evaluate test behavior at the automatic level, to see how the child performs on more definitive speech tests, and to see if poor verbal expression is part of a larger pattern of difficulty such as a total auditory-vocal channel proble.n or a generalized expressive-process problem.

A child who shows a marked deficit in expressing himself verbally on the ITPA will perhaps answer questions with one-word answers or not at all, or he may answer specific questions but fail to divulge what information he does know on more open-ended questions where he has to initiate ideas. He may rely on gestures to express himself, and he seldom adds much to class discussion, although he may contribute if given sufficient time and a little prompting.

He may or may not show a good receptive vocabulary. Sometimes he comprehends rather complicated language but is at a loss for words in expressing himself orally. Because of their adequate understanding of class discussions these children will occasionally raise a hand to answer questions but then stumble and give an inadequate response or even no response at all.

Many of these children would rather draw a picture or demonstrate with their hands or show how a thing is done than tell about it. The young child may point but say nothing or he may spill out a few disconnected words. The older child can sometimes express himself well on paper but does poorly in oral work.

Most teachers have had a few children who appear dull but who, on closer acquaintance, exhibit knowledge and acumen which ranks them above the average of the class. Often these children have difficulty expressing themselves. At the other extreme are those children who talk a lot but have little to say. They may give off a lot of static, a lot of irrelevant chatter, and much repetition, but few relevant concepts. Both of these kinds of children would probably score low on the Verbal Expression test.

Manual expression

Manual expression is the ability to express an idea or ideas with hand gestures. It taps a broad ability in nonverbal expression which includes facial expression and other bodily movements and subtle gestures. It should not be confused with manual dexterity or gross motor coordination, for even a cerebral-palsied child with poor control of hands and body can sometimes get an idea across with clumsy but understandable movements. A perfect example of manual expression is the use of the manual language or finger spelling by the deaf. When this is learned it becomes a substitute for verbal expression.

The principal implication of a manual expression deficit is that of central involvement, not peripheral motor ability. The test evaluates motor activity in terms of the intent to express an idea as well as the actual physical expression.

Manual expression (or its broader counterpart of general motor expression) does require a certain degree of manipulative skill and central control of the routine acts of bodily movement. These are acts and movements which have been acquired at the automatic level of organized and integrated responses. If they are not present, the child may have difficulty at the meaningful level of manual expression. It does not follow, however, that a child who has good motor coordination and is skilled in manipulation of objects, such as batting a ball or putting pegs in a hole, will necessarily be competent in manual expression.

Further checks to determine support or doubt of a manual expression disability might include the formboard and block-building subtests of the Binet at the younger ages, the Goodenough Draw-a-Man Test (Goodenough, 1962; Harris, 1963), and the Money Road Map Test (1965). Manual expressive ability may also affect responses to some tests purported to measure visual perception such as the Bender Gestalt, the Developmental Test of Visual-Motor Integration (1967), and the reproduction of forms on the Stanford-Binet and the Ontario School Ability Examination (1936). If a child lacks a sense of laterality, directionality, spatial orientation, and/or body image, he will usually be limited in ability on the Manual Expression subtest and restricted in his expressive motor abilities. The Purdue Perceptual Rating Survey (Kephart, 1960) may be helpful here in tracing specific areas which may need development prior to or parallel to training in manual expression or broader areas of motor expression.

In the classroom children who are not "motor-minded" would rather tell you verbally than show you how something is done. They often lack facial as well as bodily expressiveness and use few gestures. They usually find it difficult to dramatize stories or play charades and pantomime activities. They may be bodily inhibited and become self-conscious when pushed into those activities which are difficult for them. They may or may not be bodily clumsy. Often there is an inadequate concept of the location of body parts and the child may misjudge the space needed for body movement, such as passing between two chairs or how high to step to get over an obstruction. He may have difficulty understanding simple maps or representing relative positions of objects on paper. He may even get lost easily in a new building because of his lack of motor-mindedness. He may have difficulty with jigsaw puzzles.

Drawing is often difficult for such a child. His pictures may be sterile and lacking in content, or they may be poorly executed. In drawing a man or a person, the child may mislocate parts of the body. He knows a man has arms but may fail to draw the torso and so put the arms coming out of the head. Likewise, his writing may be illegible or it may have poor content. Often a young child with a manual expression deficit may avoid coloring or block-building activities although he may be very active in more robust games and sometimes is very well coordinated in gross motor activities.

Children who express themselves poorly with their hands may have a dearth of ideas to express or may lack the imagination required to demonstrate the ideas so another person will understand. For example, in playing house one child may not think of many activities to perform, whereas another child may think about sweeping the floor and setting the table and rocking the baby but carry out the activities in such a cursory manner that an observer would not recognize the content. Or such a child might verbalize the activities or tell another child to do them.

Auditory closure abilities
(Grammatic Closure,
Auditory Closure,
and Sound Blending subtests)

The function which the ITPA attempts to tap here has been called auditory closure and the three tests which seem to contain this function are Grammatic Closure, Auditory Closure, and Sound Blending. These tests were devised in an attempt to tap the ability to perceptually integrate wholes from the input of partial information—to internalize what is heard over and over again. Each of these three subtests attempts to tap this function in its own unique way.

In the Grammatic Closure test an attempt has been made to test the degree to which a child has acquired automatic habits for handling syntax and grammatic inflections. The young child may fail to use verb tenses or plurals or idioms in an acceptable manner. He may speak of a "mop" as a "mopper" or an "iron" as an "ironer," both of which have a logical basis but do not follow the customary form. At this automatic level of functioning, the child learns what is habitual or customary rather than what is logical.

The verbalized rules of grammar are not important. The grammar itself is not important. The meaning is not important, for the function we are dealing with here is at the automatic level and deals with a highly integrated automatic response rather than a meaningful interpretation of symbols. The grammar is merely a medium through which to observe the ease with which a child utilizes the redundancies of his experience to learn to predict and use common verbal expressions.

A child who has difficulty in this area not only has trouble learning plurals and past tenses and irregular forms of verbs but he may mispronounce words he has heard many times; he may put the verb or adjective in the wrong place or tangle up parts of words in "spoonerisms" or "malapropisms" like "Let me sew you to your sheet" instead of "Let me show you to your seat"; or "I pledge a leash unto the flag" rather than "I pledge allegiance to the flag."

He may have difficulty learning nursery rhymes, learning to count, learning multiplication facts by rote, learning to tell time, learning his teacher's or the children's names. He needs much repetition to learn these things. This difficulty is commonly associated with speech problems because the child has not learned from the redundancies of his environment.

When ability on the Grammatic Closure test is below other abilities, one must check to make sure the difficulty is not traceable to an inability to make the auditory discrimination between alternatives (such as "open, opened," "write, wrote," "men, man"), before assuming the source of the difficulty to be in the ability to predict and use these forms. If he does not differentiate them auditorily, he will be unable to utilize them vocally. Likewise, a difficulty in discrimination may be traceable to poor auditory acuity, which should be checked.

As has been noted earlier, interpretation of a low score on the Grammatic Closure test should take into account the language to which the child is exposed. In some subcultures word endings are commonly slurred over or regular plurals are used where irregular plurals are grammatically correct. Since the ITPA was standardized on a mainly Caucasian population, all colloquial patterns should be noted.

The supplementary Auditory Closure test attempts to measure the phenomenon of closure in a different way. It attempts to measure the child's ability to grasp a word when only part of the word is presented to him. He must utilize closure to recognize the word. It is the same kind of ability needed to grasp a telephone conversation when there are background noises interfering and blotting out part of the sounds heard. It is probably related to the ability to understand speech with a foreign accent or poorly articulated speech.

The Sound Blending test attacks the phenomenon of auditory closure from the point of view of synthesis and the ability to integrate isolated sounds into a whole word. It is a much-needed operation in learning to utilize a phonic approach to reading and, normally, can be readily taught. If the child is deficient in this function, however, he may experience considerable difficulty in learning to hear isolated sounds and perceive them as parts of a whole.

The child who has not acquired this facility may know all of the sounds of letter symbols and yet not be able to read because he cannot synthesize the sounds into a word. He may sound only the first symbol or two in a word and guess at the rest. He finds it difficult to make use of phonic instruction and cannot attack new words independently, although he may be able to learn sight words fairly well.

These three tests, along with other tests at the automatic level, are very relevant to school success. Research has shown difficulty on them to be correlated with difficulty in school. Articulatory speech defects are likewise correlated with these auditory tests at the automatic level. Perhaps failure to auditorize a word adequately or to be able to predict what a word should sound like makes it difficult to form the word.

Visual closure

Visual closure is the ability to recognize a visual whole from the presentation of a part or of mutilated parts. Like auditory closure, it is automatically triggered. According to Thurstone (1940), visual closure includes several kinds of stimulus tasks: (a) the ability to form a meaningful figure from what initially appears to be an unorganized and scattered visual presentation. In this kind of closure, the scattered items fall into place to form a whole; (b) the ability to select a figure when part of the figure is imbedded in another figure or when the figure is mutilated by extraneous marks; (c) the ability to select a figure by discarding parts of the stimulus. In other words, obtaining closure does not require using all the elements in the visual field.

In practice one derives a whole percept from a presentation of part of the figure or isolated or contaminated parts, such as recognizing a cat from the presentation of only part of the cat, extracting the image of a cat from a confusing figure-ground stimulus, or automatically envisaging a cat when the parts are isolated or disoriented. It is the automatic tendency to alter a perception in such a way that it fits a visual image. The readiness with which these pieces fall into place may determine one's speed of perception.

The visual closure test of the Minnesota Preschool Scale would be another test by which to assess this function. On the WISC both object assembly and block designs probably involve considerable visual closure ability as does the coding test, which involves paired associate learning at the automatic level. Finding missing parts as in the picture completion test of the WISC may be somewhat related in that the child must identify the incomplete picture. The manikin subtest of the WISC also involves visual closure.

Auditory sequential memory

Auditory sequential memory is short-term, nonmeaningful memory enabling the individual to remember a sequence of auditory stimuli long enough to repeat them or otherwise make use of them. In evaluating the score on this test it would be wise to check the child's ability to learn his telephone number and street address at a reasonable age, his ability to learn jingles, poems, prayers, etc., and his ability to repeat digits as presented on the Binet and WISC tests. Memory for sentences on the Binet (year IV, alternate) is contaminated with meaning and is not a pure rote memory test, but often a child with difficulty on the Auditory Sequential Memory test of the ITPA will repeat the idea without repeating the exact words, or he may be unable to repeat the sentence in spite of understanding the content.

The factor of sustained attention may affect a child's short-term auditory memory and should be taken into account in any further diagnosis. Apparent anxiety, hyperactivity, or distractability could lower the score on this test. The ability as tested by the ITPA does not involve meaningful memory, for it is an automatic response to sounds and can be evoked by nonsense syllables or foreign words or isolated letters just as well. Neither do the test results imply ability in long-term memory.

The child with poor auditory sequential memory may be poor in spelling, and if he goes up to the teacher to ask how to spell a word, he may not be able to remember it long enough to get back to his seat and write it down. He often gets the sounds or syllables of a word twisted, reverses number or letter sequences, or cannot remember instructions long enough to execute them. He may be poor in phonics because he cannot remember the sounds long enough to blend them.

He often has a history of not being able to learn his address, nursery rhymes, counting, or the alphabet. It is not uncommon for him to have had a delay in speech and articulation. Sometimes he tries to repeat things to himself in order to rehearse them so he can remember.

Visual sequential memory

Visual sequential memory is short-term memory for a visual sequence. Like auditory memory, it is an ability at the automatic level not requiring understanding of the figures or objects in the sequence. The task is sometimes facilitated or circumvented by using mnemonic devices involving meaning or by verbalizing so as to utilize auditory memory.

The Knox Cubes Test is a good check of nonmeaningful visual sequential memory, although it includes a motor component. Monroe's (1932) visual memory test for nonsense syllables and forms assesses the child's ability to remember sequences of nonmeaningful discrete stimuli. The Ontario School Ability Examination contains several subtests involving visual, motor, and perhaps haptic sequencing: the dominoes test, the Knox Cubes Test, the tapping test are sensitive to this ability.

One determining factor in poor visual sequential memory ability may be a correlated visualization problem. Some evidence is available suggesting a positive relationship between memory for letters and reading level (Sutton, 1963). The trainability of visualizing ability by using the kinesthetic method of teaching reading was suggested by an experiment by Hirsch (1963).

The presence of a visual memory deficit in the classroom may be quite obvious. The child frequently shows reversals in reading and spelling, in writing his name, in recognizing sight words, in finding the right page number. He cannot remember a word or a series of numbers long enough to get to the blackboard to write it. In reading, he is quite dependent on phonics and often remembers items better if he can say them out loud or write them down.

Summary—an integrative statement

The present twelve ITPA subtests do not cover all the psycholinguistic areas shown in the more complete communication model presented in this chapter. Nor do these tests take into account problems of personality, mental set, emotional disturbance, or physical abnormalities. They are an attempt to measure certain perceptual and cognitive abilities which seem to bear a relationship to intellectual development and academic learning. For this reason and because of the need for the more precise pinpointing of deficits and correlated areas of possible weaknesses, supplementary diagnostic procedures have been suggested. More will be discovered by the astute diagnostician.

Some children show such clear-cut areas of marked deficiency that a detailed remedial program can be outlined with little supplementary diagnosis. The procedures suggested in this section are most often helpful and necessary in borderline cases or in cases where the deficiencies are not clear-cut.

The diagnostician must keep in mind, above all else and as a guideline to all diagnostic procedures, that the purpose of making a diagnosis is to plan a remedial program. The remedial program which results should be grounded at every point in the findings derived from an adequate diagnosis. However, the processes of diagnosis and remediation are not as separate and artificial as they have been made here. Actually, the child's response to remedial techniques can provide further useful diagnostic information. Diagnosis and remediation thus cannot and should not be separated in philosophy or practice. Diagnosis should be an ongoing process.

Chapter eight

General guidelines for remediation

Most textbooks on teaching deal with the imparting of knowledge and the acquisition of skills or proficiencies. They offer basic principles for sound teaching practices: showing success at every step in the teaching process, using minimal steps of increasing difficulty, providing for overlearning, spacing practice, providing for periodic review, providing for appropriate reinforcement, avoiding overloading and retroactive and proactive inhibition. These are vitally important principles for all learning, whether performed in a group situation or individually. They should be continually utilized and frequently reviewed by the teacher.

Beyond these general principles of good teaching the present chapter focuses on guidelines which are less frequently discussed and sometimes controversial. They are derived from the central thesis of this book and apply mainly to the remediation of deficiencies which obstruct the acquisition of information and the development of skills and proficiencies.

Differentiate testing from teaching

Testing seeks to determine what a child can and cannot do. Teaching seeks to develop the skills necessary to fulfill the goals of education. A remedial teacher conducts both of these operations and should be aware of which one she is performing. Oftentimes in classroom instruction what passes for teaching is in reality testing. When a teacher merely asks a child a question, she is testing him. If the child succeeds, she knows he can perform that function; if he fails, she knows he cannot. When a teacher asks a child to read the word "dog," she is testing him. If the child fails, the teacher has gained some information about what the child can and cannot do. If she then tells him the word, she is prompting him, which is teaching. If he succeeds and she repeats his response with approval, she is also teaching him by confirmation, and her reinforcement makes it more likely that the child will know that word the next time.

In remediation the teacher alternately tests and teaches, or teaches and tests. There is a circular relationship between evaluation and remediation, for as the teacher works with a child, she is constantly diagnosing. Thus, diagnosis leads to remediation and remediation leads to diagnosis.

The teacher tests the child to find out if he can perform a particular task. She utilizes his response as feedback to determine her next step. If he fails, she makes the task simpler or breaks it down into component parts until he can perform the separate aspects of the task and then integrate them into the whole. This requires considerable analysis on the part of the teacher to become aware of the basic elements of a particular task. It may be necessary, as in experimental behavior analysis, to observe the child's response to a series of situations and note where he succeeds and where he fails.

In teaching, a child should never be left in a failure. But in formal testing one is not concerned with whether or not a child fails. The failure gives a measure of the child's ability but does nothing to remedy it. In testing, the examiner does not make it easier for the child, nor is the child told to do it again unless that is an integral part of the test. In teaching, tasks are geared to the child's ability, or slightly beyond. Then if he fails, he is given help and hopefully acquires new knowledge or a new ability, leaving him with a feeling of success.

Another difference between testing and teaching is that testing is discrete whereas teaching is integrative. In diagnostic testing to determine a child's ability in discrete areas, it is necessary to provide a situation and a task which test only that specific ability. In other words, in testing a child's ability to hear, visual clues by which he might achieve the accepted response are eliminated. In examining his ability to see relationships in pictures, nothing is verbalized for him. Admittedly, there is no such thing as absolute isolation of abilities, but tasks can be presented which minimize the use of other functions. On the ITPA, for example, when testing one function the requirements in other areas are held at a low level. In the Auditory Reception test the visual requirements are eliminated entirely; the expressive requirements are held to a two-year-old level; automatic-level contamination is minimized through psychometric procedures and excluding variations in syntax.

Contrary to this procedure, teaching does not eliminate the use of abilities other than the one needing development. Teaching is not discrete but integrative. Activities which promote the development of verbal expression, for example, also involve the use of auditory reception, memory, and association as well as visual and other functions. It is the task of the teacher to integrate verbal expression activities with these other functions and thereby draw verbal expression into the mainstream of the child's functioning. Games which involve verbal give-and-take may not tax a child's auditory reception, but by integrating auditory reception with the requirement of verbal expression, the child is assisted in the ability to express himself.

Train the deficient areas

There has been some controversy as to whether to utilize a child's assets or train his deficits. It appears that much of this controversy is more apparent than real for it is not an either/or question. It is necessary to use the assets and also train the deficits. Current thinking today does not hold that deficits are innate and unalterable. If they were, then, of course, we could rely solely on assets. But on the assumption that most learning disabilities can be ameliorated, it is advisable to develop abilities which are not functioning adequately. Disregarding a deficit and developing other abilities to take its place is compensation. If a child is deaf and his deafness cannot be cured, the child is educated through other sense modalities. This is compensation. If, on the other hand, the child has some hearing, an attempt is made to ameliorate the deficit through hearing aids and auditory training. Similarly, physical rehabilitation is used extensively with postpolio patients and only where further development has failed are compensatory methods used.

History has provided many examples of corrective methods used to improve the weak areas by men who have subsequently overcome their defects. The Greek orator Demosthenes and Teddy Roosevelt are notable examples. They found their weaknesses and set about training those areas, not compensating with other abilities. Demosthenes struggled to overcome a speech impediment by learning to talk with pebbles in his mouth. Roosevelt pushed himself into a rugged ranch life and overcame his frailty. Compensating for disabilities by utilizing assets, on the other hand, has definite disadvantages. By bypassing activities in which the child does poorly and providing activities in which he does well, the child's discrepancies between abilities become exaggerated. Weak areas remain weak while strong areas become stronger. This often happens at home when parents "show off" a child in activities in which he does well and overlook activities in which he does poorly. One child may develop verbal fluency or expression at the expense of motor expression. He obtains reinforcement from his parents and teachers for verbal activities and tends to avoid motor expressive activities which he does poorly and for which he receives no approval or reinforcement. Hence, many of the psycholinguistic deficits found in children are, at least partly, the result of lack of experience and encouragement in those areas during the child's early development.

It is interesting to note that among the culturally different or economically disadvantaged we find some deficits which are probably due to disuse and lack of training rather than to neurological origins. How irreversible these deficits are remains to be seen. It seems reasonable to expect, however, that early attempts at alleviating these deficits will bear fruit. Even among those whose disabilities are neurologically related it is likely that the behavioral deficits become exaggerated because of avoidance and can be improved through remediation (Kirk, 1967).

Remedial programs aim, therefore, to stimulate the functioning of those abilities in which the child is below par. Even if those abilities cannot be brought up to average functioning, experience has shown that they can usually be improved and the gap can be reduced between them and the child's more successful areas which he continues to exercise without special help.

Utilize areas of strength

The urgency for training deficits in a child does not mean that assets are disregarded. On the contrary, assets are very important and have some very specific uses in the process of remediation.

Over and above the fact that the child is going to use and develop these areas of strength spontaneously, such areas serve an important role in the teaching process. In the first place, there are many situations whereby he can acquire knowledge through his stronger channel or by use of substitute strategies. In social studies, for example, if a child cannot read printed material or is slow in comprehending oral material, such visual aids as filmstrips may be necessary for him to keep up in a classroom situation. Such methods can be used concurrently with training to correct the deficiencies in his weak areas. In other words, while the deficits are being remediated in certain periods his general education tends to use his assets for other purposes.

In the second place, the assets are used to develop weaker areas. Following are some examples wherein strengths are used to modify weaknesses.

1. If a child has low auditory reception but high visual reception, auditory reception is developed by presenting a visual stimulus the child understands to give meaning to the comparable auditory stimulus which he does not understand. Later the auditory stimulus is presented alone. For example, if a child does not understand such commands as "Wiggle your fingers," "Raise your hand," "Pick up your pencil," etc., the remedial exercise could consist of Simple Simon games or their variations. Thus, a teacher says "Simple Simon says 'Wiggle your finger,' " and at the same time wiggles her finger but draws attention to the verbal command. The child imitates what he sees. After other directions or commands are made with the visual counterpart, the remedial teacher says "Simple Simon says 'Wiggle your finger' " without using the visual clue for imitation. In this teaching situation the child learns to follow the auditory command without the visual clue for imitation. He has learned to "hear and do"; i.e., he has learned to interpret what he hears in order to perform the action.

2. Adequate receptive ability can be used to elevate the verbal expressive ability. In this case, the auditory receptive ability will be used to help him to "hear and say," his visual reception to "see and say," and his kinesthetic reception to "do and say."

3. If the child can repeat sentences but is unable to spontaneously express ideas, the teacher uses the ability to repeat in developing the ability to express, such as showing the child a ball and saying "This is a ball. Say 'This is a ball.' " When the child responds, the

teacher says "What is this?" and expects the child to respond "This is a ball."

4. If a child has difficulty seeing relationships in the area of auditory association but grasps such relationships in the visual association area, the latter relationships may be shown in conjunction with the auditory presentation. For example, if the teacher asks the child how a kitten and a puppy are alike, it might be necessary to also show him pictures of a big cat and a kitten and of a dog and a little puppy. The visual relationships can then be noted and the more subtle relationships of age and family similiarities demonstrated. Then, without using pictures, a similar situation can help the child understand relationships verbally, gradually extending the task to more varied relationships.

"What goes with a hammer?" (No response.)

The child is shown several items or pictures of items. "Which of these goes with a hammer?" (He points to the nail.)

"What is that?"

"A nail."

"You tell me what goes with a hammer."

"The nail."

The items are removed and the original question repeated. "What goes with a hammer?"

Hopefully, this time the child will answer correctly without the visible objects. If not, he may be asked to recall what those other things were that he looked at. Or the question may be simplified by asking "Does a nail or a sponge go with the hammer?"

These illustrations do not imply that the training of all deficits must rely on assets. In some situations the training of a deficit, like sound blending, may have to be accomplished directly with specially designed exercises.

Use multisensory presentations appropriately

Some controversy has arisen in regard to the use of multisensory stimulation in contrast to a unisensory presentation. The appropriate use of multisensory presentation depends on the disability of the child, on what one is trying to accomplish, and on the stage of development of the child. To assume that training in one sense modality will transfer to another sense modality in children with disabilities is not always sound. On the other hand, assuming that multisensory stimulation will increase learning ability in all cases is likewise questionable.

With some children the stimulus in one sense modality may interfere with reception in another sense modality. It may become just a distraction and serve to confuse the child who is relying on another modality of reception. If he lacks the ability to interpret what he receives in one sense modality, he will switch to a sense modality through which it is easier for him to make use of the stimuli. When he is unable to shut out the confusing stimuli from his weaker area, it serves as so much "noise" which interferes with the adequate functioning of any channel. Only when the information received from both channels can be integrated is a multisensory presentation of value in remediation.

Some children learn better through a visual modality, others learn better through an auditory modality, while others benefit most from a tactile or kinesthetic modality. Soviet psychologists refer to neuropsychological counterparts as visual analyzers, auditory analyzers, or kinesthetic (or motor) analyzers. In the intact organism these analyzers are integrated. In pathological conditions there is disintegration.

With normally developing children the simultaneous use of more than one sense field probably serves to intensify the reception of information, with the presentation of stimuli in one modality serving as an adjunct to other modalities. Multisensory approaches in teaching are, therefore, common and usually helpful. When a classroom teacher faces twenty to thirty children, some of whom undoubtedly comprehend material presented in one channel better than in another, she often uses audio and/or visual aids and sometimes tactual-kinesthetic aids to supplement the usual classroom presentation. This multisensory approach provides an opportunity for all children to acquire the information through their best modality. It provides added stimulation for the child who uses all channels equally well. It also helps to integrate the analyzers (to borrow the Russian term).

Indiscriminate bombardment of multisensory stimulation is, however, a shotgun approach and is not the best way of using multisensory media with many children who exhibit divergent learning abilities. The very reason for presenting ordinary children with various forms of sensory input is to make sure that they receive the information through one sense modality or another. In a classroom situation where the child who is weak in one receptive function is struggling to keep up with the rest of the class, the multisensory presentation is a real boon because it allows him to use the channel in which he functions best. He often completely disregards the use of other modalities. In remediation this is just what we *do not* want, for the child is thereby exercising that which he already has and further weakening the deficient function through disuse.

In remedial work multisensory media are also used but they are used judiciously. They are used in such a way as to help the child make use of the *weak* receptive function, thereby learning how to gain meaning through that channel. If a child has difficulty picking up a sequence of beats on the drum or knocks on the door, the teacher may help the sequence take form by presenting a comparable graphic pattern in the visual channel. Seeing these patterns visually and having them presented simultaneously with, or in immediate succession to, the auditory stimuli gives the child a point-to-point correspondence between the two sensory stimuli. But the presentation is not dropped at this point for the child has not yet taxed his auditory recognition of the pattern. The same pattern must next be presented without the visual stimulus. Dependence on the intact function should be gradually faded out. Continued dependence on reception in the intact area would defeat the purpose by allowing the child to use this area to the neglect of the area being remediated.

One child was diagnosed as having intact auditory abilities but very deficient visual abilities. To teach this child to read, the parent wrote words on flash cards and presented them to the child as follows: "This is k-i-t-t-e-n (saying each letter), kitten. Say 'kitten.' " By this process, spelling each word as it was presented to the child visually, the child learned thirty words. Upon examination by one of the authors it was found that the child could recall all of the words when spelled without the visual presentation but could not read any of the thirty words when presented visually without the auditory cues of saying each letter. This is a multisensory approach, but the child learned only through unisensory stimulation in the auditory channel. In this case the child paid attention only to the auditory stimulation and disregarded the visual stimulus. By altering the instructional procedure and gradually fading out the auditory stimulus the child learned to read by a visual approach.

In certain situations unisensory stimulation is necessary. If a child, for example, has a disability in sound blending and has had difficulty in learning to read, remediation should be initially through auditory sound blending training without reliance on visually presented letters. The child must ultimately learn to blend sounds presented auditorily. When this is accomplished he then learns visual symbols of phonemes, and through auditory and/or subvocal clues is able to automatically sound the phonemes and blend them into the word.

Most learning is intersensory. The young child experiences a cat tactually, visually, auditorily, kinesthetically. Then he learns to understand the vocal symbol "cat" which revives images of the previous experience. Later he learns to recognize the visual symbol "cat" in reading; all these sensory experiences are interrelated. The young child learns visual space through motor experiences. He may reach for a ball which is too far away. He crawls toward it, reaches again, crawls and reaches, until he comes into contact with the ball. Through such experiences he learns to judge distance. Similarly, in the normally developing child auditory language is learned within the framework of visual and kinesthetic experiences; later attaching meaning to visual symbols in reading is related to the understanding of auditory symbols. Thus, the judicious use of multisensory presentations and cross-modality techniques are valuable in remediation. When to use unisensory and multisensory approaches in remediation depends upon the tolerance of the child and his response to the stimulations. These cannot be generalized but can be determined by a competent diagnostic-remedial teacher.

The program of remediation that is to be designed must necessarily determine (a) whether the auditory, visual, or kinesthetic analyzer should be used in isolation, (b) whether one should be developed with the aid of the other two, or (c) whether remediation should integrate the analyzers to function in unison. An analysis of the child's responses should give clues to the most effective approach for the child at his stage of development. The ultimate target, of course, is to produce an integration of the analyzers to function simultaneously and as a unit.

Remediate prerequisite deficits first

In organizing a remedial program for a child it is necessary to decide whether one deficit is basic to another. An extremely defective auditory receptive ability may be associated with poor auditory association and verbal expression. The remedial program in such a case should emphasize the development of auditory reception and integrate it with auditory association and verbal expression. A child who is low in both verbal expression and auditory memory may have as his basic deficiency auditory memory. During the developmental stages he may have been unable to imitate sentences in his environment because of a very deficient short-term memory. Remediation in his case should be on memory training in relation to words, phrases, and sentences, prior to or in conjunction with determining meaning from auditory symbols. The aim of the remediation is to assist him in keeping in mind a sentence which he has just heard so that he can repeat and interpret it.

Poor visual reception may be dependent upon poor visual discrimination. It may be necessary to develop an awareness of figure-ground relationships, spatial orientation, visual closure, or form discrimination. Poor auditory reception may be based on poor auditory discrimination. The child has not learned to understand spoken language because speech sounds are not differentiated. If the sounds are not differentiated, perhaps the sounds are not clearly heard because of a slight hearing loss. Such problems should be traced back to prerequisite deficits.

The purpose of a diagnosis, as indicated in Chapters 5, 6, and 7, is not only to look at the lowest score in the profile and organize a program for its improvement. It is to look at the *pattern* of abilities and disabilities, to evaluate the correlates, and to evolve a diagnostic hypothesis. This diagnostic hypothesis should indicate where to start and what deficiency or deficiencies to remediate first. If it is hypothesized, for example, that the child does not talk because he does not understand oral language, then it is obvious that auditory reception should be the basic area to remediate. The child is not going to learn to express himself verbally unless he understands the symbols to be used.

Make provisions for utilizing feedback

Good teaching makes use of three general forms of feedback: (a) the feedback the teacher receives from the child when he answers a question or completes a lesson, (b) the feedback the child receives from the teacher when she is confirming or correcting his response, and (c) the internal or external feedback the child receives from his own actual and covert responses, vocal or motor.

Remedial instruction in a one-to-one tutoring situation emphasizes continual feedback between the child and the teacher for the purpose of correcting the child's responses to the task in hand.

The internal and external feedback in which the child, instead of the teacher, monitors his own responses is very important in learning. When a teacher, for example, asks a child to repeat a sentence, the child (a) receives the stimulus auditorily, (b) associates it internally with his past experience, (c) responds verbally, correctly or incorrectly, and (d) receives the stimulus of his response auditorily (external feedback) and internally through vocal or subvocal muscle response or proprioception. He can monitor his own response in order to recognize the error and respond correctly. Feedback provides a self-correctional device if the individual recognizes his errors. Self-instructional programmed material provides for feedback and self-correction.

Some systems of remediation of deficits are based on a built-in feedback system. Kephart (1960) bases his system on what he calls the perceptual-motor generalization which must match the motor activity to the perceptual activity. The motor response becomes in part an internalized feedback mechanism and serves to integrate the motor and the perceptual activities. In learning to make correct responses the child uses feedback as a control so that if the response is incorrect, the circular sequence of output, input (feedback), output continues until the motor response matches the perceptual information.

An excellent example of feedback and correction is found in the Fernald (1943) system of teaching reading. The child sees a word or phrase, then from memory tries to reproduce the word or phrase, checks with the model, and, if incorrect, tries again. He continues monitoring his own responses until there is a match between the model he sees and his written response.

In organizing a remedial program provision should be made for vocal and/or motor response when appropriate so that the child will obtain internal and external feedback. Experiments have shown, for example, that a child can learn a list of words more efficiently if he vocalizes the words than if he does not. He will learn and retain them better if he vocalizes and writes the words. In other words, remedial programs should have a built-in response (vocal or motor) and a situation in which the child will have a chance to monitor his own responses and correct them.

Develop abilities functionally

It is preferable to develop abilities in a natural, everyday situation rather than in an artificial setting, and to train abilities directly in the performance that is required.

There are on the market today many workbooks and exercises designed to develop specific functions in children. It is the duty of the remedial teacher to analyze these materials and to examine whether the tasks included are going to transfer to a desired activity. For example, if a child has problems in visual discrimination and needs this ability to learn to discriminate letters and words, it is preferable to organize activities that would discriminate letters and words rather than activities that are designed to discriminate circles and squares. If a child has had difficulty in learning to read and if he shows defective visual sequential ability (which has been shown to be related to reading disabilities), it is preferable to train visual sequential ability with letters, words, and phrases.

In training a specific ability it is preferable to utilize training that is transferable and usable in a life situation. If a child lacks verbal expression and is receiving tutoring to develop words and sentences, he will progress faster if the lessons provide functional words that are used in the home and in the school.

Start remedial programs early

There is considerable evidence from preschool education and from ideographic research that early remediation for young children with learning disabilities produces better results than initiating programs at a later age. The earlier practice was to allow a child to fail for a number of years at home and at school and provide remediation only after he became a problem. Unfortunately, this practice is still common.

An ideal situation would identify these children in nursery school and kindergarten, at the latest during the first and second grades. Remediation of learning disabilities at that age level could prevent failures in many of these children at school and in life. Many school dropouts are cases of learning disabilities.

Individualize instruction

Remediation of learning disabilities is necessarily an individualized program. Placing a heterogeneous group of children with different learning disabilities in one class with one teacher and with one method of remediation will not be successful. The unique disabilities found in each child require that the remedial method be tailored for that child alone and not for a group. There are a number of organizational procedures that have been used to facilitate individual instruction. Some of the more common procedures follow.

1. *The itinerant diagnostic-remedial teacher plan.* Under this system the child with a learning disability remains in his regular grade but is tutored by a diagnostic-remedial teacher for half an hour to one hour a day. In addition to offering the child remediation for his particular disability, the remedial teacher attempts to fit the child into the regular class program by supplying the regular teacher with suggestions and materials. The goal of the remedial teacher is to correct or ameliorate the disability so that the child can progress and adjust to the regular school program without continuing individual instruction. Under this plan one remedial teacher can serve five to eight children in several schools.

2. *The resource room plan.* This plan is similar to the itinerant teacher plan in that the child is assigned to a regular class and goes to the resource room for individual remediation of his disability. In this plan the diagnostic-remedial teacher remains in one room with materials and equipment and offers remediation to children on an individual or small-group basis for two to three children needing the same type of help. Under this plan a remedial teacher can serve eight to twelve children in one school building and can consult with the regular teachers on the classroom program for these and other children.

3. *The individualized class.* Another form of organization is to assign six to eight learning disability children to one teacher for the whole day. In such a class the teacher conducts some group activities but the bulk of the day is devoted to tutoring individuals. The teacher works with one child for a half hour and then gives the child independent work on the remedial lesson. While the other children are doing their seat work, usually programmed, the teacher tutors another child individually. Under this plan the program of remediation and seat work is individually tailored to the remedial needs of each child.

4. *The two-teacher class.* Under this plan one regular teacher and one remedial teacher are assigned to a class of ten to fifteen chil-

dren. While one teacher conducts group activities following the curriculum of the regular grades, the remedial teacher gives remedial tutoring to individual children. This plan has the advantage of more adequately integrating remedial lessons with regular work and applies only to a large school.

Chapter nine

Specific guidelines for remediation

The purpose of this chapter is to offer guidelines for the development of remedial procedures for the various functions measured by the ITPA. The chapter does not develop these procedures; it is not a curriculum or a course of study or a step-by-step sequence of activities for remediation. It is, rather, an endeavor to guide the remedial teacher in developing her own procedures for each child by giving her a broader understanding of the ten areas evaluated by the test and a further analysis of what each task involves. A child may fail to perform a particular task for any one of a number of reasons. In auditory reception, for example, a child may fail to understand what is said to him because he fails to recognize and identify words. He may even fail to identify and recognize other environmental sounds. He may not attend to auditory stimuli. He may not have attached meaning to isolated words. Or he may know the separate words but have difficulty understanding consecutive speech. In a practical situation auditory reception covers a much broader area than just answering "yes" or "no" to the particular questions presented on the test.

It is hoped that the breakdown of tasks presented in this chapter will help the teacher analyze the child's failure in a particular task so that she may help him develop the requisite abilities. By studying the various tasks outlined under each function in this chapter, the teacher may be aided in the selection or development of activities that will remediate the disability.

It should also be pointed out that in breaking down the ten areas, some of the abilities listed fall into a developmental sequence, but others represent diverse aspects of the task and may contain varying degrees of attainment within that aspect of the task. In manual/ motor expression, for example, three types of difficulty have been noted: the child may lack basic motor skills; he may lack ideas leading to motor expression; or he may not make his ideas operational. The teacher, then, is asked to make further diagnosis of the child's functioning to find out why the tasks presented are difficult for him or what particular facets of the function cause him trouble. She will then have a better idea of where to direct her efforts. In considering relevant techniques of remediation for a particular child, the teacher must relate her techniques not only to the particular area of weakness but also to the child's level of development in that particular area and also in other areas of functioning.

As indicated in Chapter 8, remediation involves the utilization of many functions in addition to the deficit requiring remediation. Although the functions have been outlined separately, teaching does not eliminate other functions when remediating the major disability or disabilities. The most effective remediation attempts to integrate the disability with other abilities. Note the following example of a teacher who is attempting to remediate a child with a significant auditory association disability.

Teacher shows the child a glass and says "What is this?"

Child: "Glass." (This required visual reception and verbal response.)

Teacher: "What do we do with a glass?"

Child: No response.

Teacher: "Do we eat it? Do we write with it? Do we drink from it?"

Child: "We drink." (This required auditory reception and verbal expression as well as auditory association.)

Teacher: "What do we drink from it?"

Child: "Water." (This required auditory reception, auditory association, and verbal expression.)

Teacher: "What else do we drink from it?"

Later: "What kinds of glasses do we have? What else do we drink from? What else do we use glasses for?"

Whatever materials are used, the teacher must ask herself, "In what levels, in what processes, in what channels does this child need development? How can this material create an activity that will alleviate the child's particular problems?" Handling materials and activities for remediation demands adaptation to steer the activity where needed. The main aim of remediation, in contrast to regular teaching, is to emphasize the instructional techniques and content that will ameliorate the disability.

The different functions tested by the ITPA can be analyzed in a number of ways, and the tasks can be analyzed in an infinite number of stages. To keep the analysis within reason the functions have been broken down as follows, presenting first the auditory-vocal functions and second the visual-motor functions.

Auditory reception

A. The child may not recognize and identify sounds in his environment.

B. The child may not have developed a listening attitude.

C. The child may have difficulty attaching meaning to words.

D. The child may not understand consecutive speech.

Auditory association

A. The child may have difficulty holding two or more concepts in mind and considering them in relation to each other.

B. The child may have difficulty identifying and verbalizing first-order relationships (directly relating two verbal concepts).

C. The child may have difficulty identifying and verbalizing second-order relationships (finding a specific relationship to match one already given).

D. The child may have difficulty learning to classify or categorize concepts.

E. The child may have difficulty finding and evaluating alternative solutions to a problem.

Verbal expression

A. The child may lack basic vocal skills.

B. The child may lack adequate vocabulary.

C. The child may not express ideas spontaneously (difficulty in retrieval of words or ideas).

D. The child may lack automatic grammatic skills.

E. The child may lack adequate interpersonal communication.

Grammatic and auditory closure

A. The child may not have had sufficient exposure to the material being presented.

B. The child may lack adequate short-term auditory memory.

C. The child may not reactivate what he hears, either vocally or subvocally.

D. The child may not learn readily even when experiences have been repeated many times.

E. The child may have difficulty synthesizing isolated sounds into words (sound blending).

Auditory sequential memory

A. The child may have difficulty attending to the details of auditory stimuli.

B. The child may have difficulty repeating what he has heard and attended to.

C. The child may have difficulty storing and retrieving information.

Visual reception

A. The child may lack prerequisite skills of visual-motor perception.

B. The child may lack knowledge and experience.

C. The child may not observe things within his visual field.

D. The child may not attach meaning to visual symbols.

E. The child may not utilize visual imagery.

Visual association

A. The child may have difficulty holding two or more concepts in mind and considering them in relation to each other.

B. The child may have difficulty identifying first-order relationships (directly relating two visual concepts).

C. The child may have difficulty identifying second-order relationships (finding a specific relationship to match one already given).

D. The child may have difficulty classifying or categorizing visual concepts.

E. The child may have difficulty finding and evaluating alternate solutions to a problem.

Manual/motor expression

A. The child may lack prerequisite perceptual-motor skills.

B. The child may lack ideas leading to motor expression.

C. The child may not make ideas operational.

Visual closure

A. The child may lack prerequisite perceptual-motor skills.

B. The child may lack the ability to visualize.

C. The child may lack the ability to organize a disparate visual field into a unified percept.

D. The child may lack adequate speed of perception.

Visual sequential memory

A. The child may show physical correlates inhibiting development of visual sequential memory.

B. The child may have difficulty attending to visual details.

C. The child may have difficulty remembering what he has seen and attended to.

D. The child may be unable to read and spell due to a visual sequential memory deficit.

E. The child may have difficulty storing and retrieving information once learned.

Building on the breakdown of abilities presented above, the following pages present suggestions for remediation and give some examples of activities which can be developed. We hope that the breakdown and suggestions for remediation will serve as guidelines for teachers in developing programs for individual children.

Auditory reception

Remediation of a deficit in auditory reception is directed toward helping the child to gain meaning from spoken language and other auditory symbols. This is a representational-level ability involving the interpretation of auditory signals which represent concepts or objects.

It should be pointed out that no sharp line can be drawn between one process and another or between one level and another. Both auditory reception and auditory association are necessary for competent functioning in the auditory channel. In normal behavior each undoubtedly triggers the other so that increased auditory association stimulates added auditory reception and vice versa. Likewise, although in normal development auditory reception precedes verbal expression, it is advisable in corrective work to combine the two processes wherever possible. Language development is best promoted by supporting one process with the other in order to obtain feedback.

The two levels of organization of communication behavior merge into each other and often function jointly. Some activities are obviously automatic in nature and others obviously involve the mediation of symbols, but many include both levels of behavior. In the suggestions which follow, some material at the automatic level has been included since many of the problems facing children with learning disabilities occur at this level. It is most important that in evaluating the abilities of their children, remedial teachers trace the difficulty through successive stages of development to see whether or not a low score on the Auditory Reception test of the ITPA is dependent on difficulty at the automatic level.

In the accompanying section, a few brief suggestions are given for improving auditory reception.

A. The child may not recognize and identify sounds in his environment

1. Teach the child to recognize a specific sound and respond when he hears it again. *Example:* Sound a buzzer and have him clap or

138

raise his hands when that particular sound is heard again. Or say a word or nonsense syllable and have him discriminate it when presented in a pair or words.

2. Make the child aware of sounds as part of his environment by:
   a. Coordinating a specific sound with its means of production. *Example:* Drop a chain of keys and then a block and note the difference in sounds. Or teach him to say an "m" sound and a "p" sound and then identify each sound with eyes closed.
   b. Identifying everyday sounds in blindfold guessing games or on tape. Each child can record a series of sounds for others to identify: running water, slamming a door, using a typewriter, vacuum cleaner, or pencil sharpener.
   c. Developing auditory figure-ground discrimination. Ask the child to respond when he hears a specific sound imbedded in background noise.
   d. Identifying classmates by their speaking voices, their singing voices, or their footsteps.
   e. Identifying emotional tones and intonations. Meaning can be indicated by intonation and inflection as well as by the actual meaning of words: (1) Garbled speech can be used to express scolding, questioning, fear, consolation, anger, etc. (2) Emphasizing the same words differently can be used to express different feelings and meanings. *Example: "What* are you doing?" "What *are* you doing?" "What are *you* doing?" "What are you *doing?"*

B. The child may not have developed a listening attitude

1. Provide motivation for listening, using tangible reinforcers and social approval in such situations as:
   a. Guessing correctly when an object has been described.
   b. Detecting such deliberate misstatements as "Ice is hot," "Dogs fly," "His voice was so loud I couldn't hear him."
   c. Following directions accurately, beginning with such simple instructions as "Give me the ball" or "Close the door" and progressing to more complicated requests.
   d. Finishing a story appropriately after listening to the first part of it. (This also stimulates auditory association and verbal expression.)

2. Prepare situations conducive to listening by:
   a. Holding the child's attention with pleasing pitch and vibrant quality which are more powerful than is intensity of the voice.
   b. Using variation in pitch, rate, and intensity to attract attention.
   c. Presenting material simply and briefly so that long periods of attention are not required.
   d. Creating exciting programs so that the child will *want* to listen.

3. Recognize that in many cases the child's receptors have been turned off by previous failures. In such cases it may be necessary to make demands far below the child's actual ability until he has developed satisfaction from success.

C. The child may have difficulty attaching meaning to words

1. Associate auditory input with pictures, actions, and motor activity. Present motor experiences simultaneously with the auditory stimulus, but emphasize the meaning of the auditory.

2. Teach a few nouns, then add action verbs, then adjectives. Begin by labeling concrete objects, using pictures where necessary. First teach words within the child's experience.

3. Teach words within categories: family members, toys, foods, colors.

4. Have the child make a vocal response even if verbal expression is inadequate. Pause occasionally before an expected word to give the child a chance to think of the word himself.

5. Have the child make a motor response as well as a verbal response to auditory stimuli wherever possible.

6. Help the child attach meaning to auditory symbols of increasing difficulty by such means as:
   a. Presenting the same words over and over until internalized, but using the words in a variety of settings and configurations rather than repetitive drill.
   b. Programming material so that new items build on previously learned material.
   c. Conditioning the child to make meaningful responses by reinforcing with tangible rewards and social approval.
   d. Limiting the vocabulary used to eliminate a lot of talking

that is meaningless to the child. Make the vocabulary meaningful by planned repetition of those words the child is to learn.

   e. Selecting the vocabulary from that vocabulary commonly used by his siblings, parents, and teachers.

7. Expand the child's concepts through auditory enrichment to give broader meaning to words in different contexts by:

   a. Reactivating experiences the child has had by conversing about past experiences.

   b. Using synonyms to expand verbal concepts.

   c. In defining objects, telling what they are *not* as well as what they are.

   d. Using words in varying contexts to give broader meaning. *Example:* "Light" refers to a lamp, to a color (light blue), to the condition of the sun (dark day, light day).

   e. Labeling and describing such abstract concepts as emotions, feelings, and intangible qualities.

   f. Through auditory association (q.v.), helping the child understand the generalized concepts of words. *Example:* "Chair" refers to desk chairs, lounge chairs, wooden chairs, metal chairs. Then pinpoint the exact meaning through context and modifiers.

D. The child may not understand consecutive speech

1. When talking to the child, be aware of such complicating factors as:

   a. Length of sentence. Perhaps the child's short-term auditory memory is weak.

   b. Separation of phrases and grouping of integral parts of the expression used. Give him time to absorb one idea at a time.

   c. Sentence structure. The child must understand simple, straightforward statements, questions, and commands before he is ready for modifying clauses and phrases, relative pronouns, or conditional clauses.

   d. Rate of speech. This includes rate of speech both within words and between words.

   e. Word emphasis. Emphasizing key words can often help to insure understanding.

2. Teach function words, prepositions, and conjunctions in phrases

with familiar words and with pictures and real-life activities (see Grammatic and Auditory Closure).

3. Teach the child to recognize words or groups of words which function as units in a sentence. In "I want a hamburger," "a" is just as much a word as "hamburger" (see Verbal Expression and Auditory Closure).

4. Develop an understanding of syntax and morphology by using planned redundancy, i.e., giving much exposure to the desired forms of language by:

a. Providing many experiences incorporating the understanding of spoken language, using supportive devices where necessary: following directions, understanding stories, understanding and answering questions, determining true-false statements, detecting deliberate misstatements, detecting verbal absurdities (auditory association), listening for specific details in a story, and finishing incomplete sentences (verbal expression).

b. Making a checklist of situations where the child does not understand spoken language. Also note errors in meaning or structure the child makes in verbal expression. Using this checklist, create situations where a particular meaning or specific language structure can be presented. Repeat a particular format using the desirable construction in these situations.

c. Teaching common expressions and language usage. Have the child repeat short sentences or phrases immediately after hearing them and then make up similar sentences with parallel structure (see Verbal Expression and Grammatic and Auditory Closure).

Auditory association

The functions of association, both visual and auditory, cover a wide field and probably encompass much of what we refer to as "reasoning," "critical thinking," and "problem-solving." The processes of both divergent and convergent thinking are probably incorporated in the ITPA process of association. Much of what Piaget calls cognitive thinking involves association (concrete operations, the ability to perceive and evaluate two dimensions, classification, evaluating sets and subsets). Many of the common activities in workbooks also require the function of association as it is hypothesized in the model of the ITPA.

In remediating a deficit in this organizing process at the representational level, an effort is made to help the child organize and integrate percepts and concepts to form new relationships. When these interrelationships are formed in the visual channel, we speak of visual association; when formed verbally, we speak of auditory association. Perhaps it is pedantic to isolate the two, for in normal cognitive behavior there is much crossing of modalities. Visual percepts and concepts often become verbalized, and verbal concepts may arouse images and interrelationships which in turn may or may not become verbalized. Likewise an auditory stimulus may activate a motor response and a visual stimulus may arouse a verbal response.

On the ITPA the process of association has been subdivided into auditory association and visual association, mainly in an effort to differentiate between the ease with which a child manipulates visual symbols and his ease in manipulating auditory symbols. The Auditory Association test presents an auditory stimulus and requires a verbal response; the Visual Association test presents visual material and requires a minimal motor response. How much translation from one modality to another occurs is difficult to determine, but what we are observing is the behavior that takes place when the materials are presented in one channel or the other.

As indicated in Chapters 5 and 6 there are many different patterns of abilities and disabilities. Some children show poor auditory reception, auditory association, and verbal expression. For these children, remediation uses activities that will develop all of the deficits. Other children may exhibit good auditory reception but low auditory association. Others may show deficits in both auditory and visual association. In each case the approach to remediation will emphasize the amelioration of the deficit, utilize the asset to develop the deficit, or select activities that will integrate reception, association, and expression.

In deciding on whether a particular activity develops reception, association, or verbal or motor expression, it is necessary to understand these processes and to interpret activities in terms of their emphasis in relation to the process that requires remediation.

The processes of reception and expression are not difficult to differentiate. A child may have adequate ability to understand the spoken word but be deficient in his ability to express his ideas. The difficult area to differentiate by observation is the difference between reception and association and between association and expression. This organizing process is one that psychology has had difficulty describing, since inferences about what goes on inside the "black box" are generally speculative. In normal development there is an integration of reception, association, and expression, and this is considered an input-mediation-output unit.

There are many games and activities that help a child in developing and understanding verbal relationships. The following suggestions offer one possible breakdown to guide the remedial teacher in finding and selecting appropriate remedial materials to cultivate this ability to organize and integrate verbal concepts.

A. The child may have difficulty holding two or more concepts in mind and considering them in relation to each other

1. When the child seems to be focusing only on one of the two concepts being related, ask him leading questions which will help him attend to one concept and then the other until he becomes aware of a relationship between them. *Example:* If the child is asked "How are a spoon and a fork alike?" he should be helped to find some parallel attributes by such suggestions as "Think of a spoon. Now think of a fork. What do you do with a spoon? What do you do with a fork? Then how are a spoon and a fork alike?"

2. Use graphic representations calling attention to the parallel aspects of the two concepts being related. "A mountain is high; a valley is ———." A visual cue may stimulate the verbal relationship. A line on the chalkboard or even a movement of the hand indicating the downward slope of the valley may suffice to bring the correct response. Later the same item should be presented without the gesture.

3. Asking the child to name objects which satisfy *two* specified requirements may help him to attend to two dimensions of the problem. *Example:* Ask him to name things which are both round *and* hard (baseball, rock, knob on gearshift of car) or round *and* not hard (orange, baby's ball) or long *and* shiny (pen, pencil, golf club, but not board, chalk, tennis shoe).

B. The child may have difficulty identifying and verbalizing first-order relationships (directly relating two verbal concepts)

1. Help the child find opposite concepts by:
   a. Demonstrating opposites first with common, tangible characteristics: up-down, hot-cold, big-little. Progress to more abstract characteristics.
   b. Testing by asking the child to supply opposites to words given; or to respond with actions opposite to what is said; or to correct you when you provide pairs that are not opposites.

2. Help the child identify differences and similarities by comparing two concepts as to function, structure, or attributes by:
   a. Asking how two concepts are different. Discuss their various attributes and functions until the child finds opposing elements. "How are milk and water different? What do you do with them? Are they liquid or solid? Are they both white?"
   b. Asking how two concepts are alike. "How are water and milk alike?" Ask leading questions as in (a).
   c. Using pictures and tangible experiences to identify likenesses and differences, helping the child to verbalize these relationships.

3. Help the child derive other kinds of relationships such as parts to the whole (child to family, an eye to a face), things commonly occurring together (nighttime and the stars, thunder and lightning), things used together (stamp and a letter, light bulb and lamp), tool and user (doctor and medicine, fireman and firetruck).

4. Help the child derive cause-and-effect relationships by:
   a. Telling or reading stories and having the child discuss why certain things happened. "What made the little boy fall down?" "What would have happened if . . . ?"
   b. Discussing and demonstrating natural events showing cause and effect. Verbalize the relationships. Use magic tricks and explain them. Conduct such simple physics experiments as putting a glass over a candle flame and explaining why it dies.
   c. Demonstrating cause and effect in social relations. Discuss what makes a child angry, happy, or frightened and what responses these situations arouse.

5. Help the child derive relationships of time and space by:
   a. Developing an awareness of time as a relationship between happenings, personal experiences, daily routines, sequences of days, seasons, past, present, and future, or between the beginning and end of an act or traversing of space.
   b. Developing an understanding of temporal relationships: before and after; pretty soon, after a while, not now; early and late, a long time and a short time; when, while, during; until; ago; tomorrow, today, yesterday; first, last, middle; beginning and end; between; next. Many of these words also relate to space and to the creation of objects, lines, and movements in space. The beginning and end of such activities can be related to both time and space.
   c. When appropriate, developing an understanding of the relationships between seconds, minutes, hours, days, etc. as divisions and subdivisions of time. Develop an appreciation of the relationship between the passage of time and the movement of the hands of the clock.
   d. Helping the child learn to relate an experience or retell a story giving the proper sequence of events.
   e. Helping the child make a meaningful sentence from three isolated words.
   f. Helping the child write a story by putting sentences in temporal order. Have each sentence on a card and read them to the child, asking him which sentence comes first, which next, which last. Begin with two sentences: "He began to cry." "Mike cut his finger."

6. Help the child derive relationships of number and space by:
   a. Clarifying the point-to-point correspondence between the

verbal and the visual and/or kinesthetic appreciation of quantity, since understanding number relationships depends on understanding relationships of objects in space. For example, seeing or feeling three beads or two beads may give the child a tangible base for understanding the verbal relationships.

b. Developing an understanding of number sequences and their quantitative relationships.

c. Helping the child understand the relationships of parts to the whole (combinations such as $2 + 2 = 4$) and of parts to parts (equivalent combinations such as $2 + 2 = 1 + 3$).

d. Providing considerable visual experience showing numerical relationships via arithmetic workbooks. These could be verbalized and related to space for the child who has difficulty in understanding space relationships verbally.

e. Helping the child understand the vocabulary of space and number: first, last; second, third; beginning, end, middle; much, little, more, less; equal, unequal; higher, lower; up, down, around, in front of, behind; long, longer, short, shorter.

C. The child may have difficulty identifying and verbalizing second-order relationships (finding a specific relationship to match one already given)

1. Help the child derive a particular relationship which is analogous to another relationship. The child must take two steps; help him by:

a. Having him identify what kind of relationship is given in a particular statement. *Example:* "Birds fly" tells how birds move. "Grass is green" tells the color of grass. "Sandpaper is rough" tells what sandpaper feels like. These are first-order relationships.

b. Then having him find a corresponding relationship applicable to a second concept. Verbal analogies are the best example of this. "Grass is green; the sky is ——." Here the child has to recognize the relationship between grass and its color, then find the corresponding relationship between the sky and its color. "The sky is far away" would be a true relationship but not analogous to the given relationship. "A rock is big; a grain of sand is ——" requires the child to find a term relative to the size of a grain of sand.

c. Identifying and matching similar relationships for both tangible and intangible concepts: function or use, structure, size, shape, color, opposites, noise made, part-whole relationships, cause-and-effect relationships, tool-user relationships.

D. The child may have difficulty learning to classify or categorize concepts

1. Help him form "sets" of objects or concepts which have some attributes in common by:
   a. Defining, as well as labeling, the class to which you want the child to respond. "Clothing," for example, might be specified as things we wear on our bodies for protection or because of custom or habit. Examples should be given of things which are not clothing like watches, rings, necklaces, keys.
   b. Testing the child's ability to place concepts in the right category. Ask him to select one of several specified categories ("Is a lion an animal or a plant?"); or name examples which fit a specified category ("Name all the animals you can think of"); or select one of several words which does not fit the same category as the others ("Which one of these does not belong with the others? Dog, candle, mouse").
   c. Helping the child define his own limits of a category. Play a simplified game of Twenty Questions. Tell the child to guess what you are thinking about. His questions should define narrower and narrower categories. "Is it alive? Is it an animal? Is it a wild animal? Is it an American animal? Does it have long fur?"

2. Help the child recognize and relate "sets" and "subsets" by:
   a. Letting the child know there are many ways of classifying the same thing. "Milk may be classified as a food but it may also be classified as a liquid." "Meat is a food but it is also a solid."
   b. Helping the child understand that there are categories within categories (sets and subsets). Have him list all the foods he can think of; then subdivide these same words in various ways: liquid or solid, from an animal or from the ground, foods he likes or dislikes, grown above ground or below ground, color, texture.
   c. Discussing animal life as divided into beasts, fish, and birds. Then play the game of Beast, Bird, or Fish.

d. Teaching the child how to tell what a word means by saying what larger category it belongs to ("A pin is something to hold things together"); or enumerating various subcategories ("There are safety pins and straight pins and decorative pins"); or distinguishing it from other members of the larger category ("A zipper and a button and a hook also hold things together but are not pins").

**E. The child may have difficulty finding
and evaluating alternative solutions
to a problem**

1. Develop ideational fluency in order to help the child see more than one possibility for relationships and solutions by:
   a. Brainstorming to stretch the child's recognition of a variety of solutions or a variety of meanings. "How many meanings are there to the word 'saw'? Of all the saws you ever saw, you never saw a saw saw like that saw that I saw saw." "How many kinds of transportation can you think of? How many ways of propelling yourself from one place to another?" "How can we find out what to feed the hamster? Look in a book; ask somebody who has one; call the pet store; try different foods." (This activity also aids verbal expression.)
   b. Accepting divergent responses with respect. They can be evaluated later.
   c. Telling incomplete stories and helping the child provide several possible endings; or possibilities of what might have happened before; or possible titles for the story.
   d. Presenting problem situations and having the child provide a variety of solutions.

2. Develop flexibility in thinking by:
   a. Cultivating the ability to take a new look at a problem or situation. Develop empathy for other individuals or for characters in a story.
   b. Developing the ability to cross from one modality to another. Translate words into movement or rhythm or pictures and vice versa.
   c. Helping the child find relationships among apparently unrelated items.

3. Develop evaluative thinking by:
   a. Helping the child learn to specify the problem or goal. If he

is finding the conclusion of a story, what problem must be solved? If he is finding a word that matches another word, what are the characteristics required? State the problem.

b. Listing various solutions and evaluating each.

c. Finding not *a* solution but the *best* solution. (The child who is easily confused by too many solutions will need extra guidance and an isolated attack on each proposal before they can be compared.)

d. Teaching the child to guess, then test his guess.

e. Using riddles and verbal absurdities to help the child apply these steps.

Verbal expression

There are various reasons that a child does not develop normally in his ability to talk. In severe cases the child may not be able to speak at all. Is it associated with poor vocal skills, i.e., poor central control of the speech mechanism? Does the child fail to understand what he hears (poor auditory reception)? Is his vocabulary inadequate? Does he have difficulty retrieving ideas to express? Does he have difficulty retrieving words to express his ideas? Is it associated with a severe deficit in auditory sequential memory or auditory closure? What level of vocal expression has he reached? Does he have a personality defect that inhibits his ability to talk? These and other questions should be answered before a systematic program of remediation is conducted. The approach that is useful and the level at which one starts depend partly on the answers to these questions.

In the following, some suggestions are offered as guidelines to the remedial teacher.

A. The child may lack basic vocal skills

1. Teach the child to imitate sounds or words. If necessary, teach imitation of motor movements or facial expressions first. Use operant techniques (see Sloane and MacAulay, 1968) to elicit those sounds the child has used in random vocalization. Then proceed to phonemes, words, and sentences by:
   a. Teaching the child to imitate the visible aspects of sound production. Use a large mirror in which the child can see both his face and the teacher's face for comparison.
   b. Teaching the child to reproduce sounds heard. Use a stereo tape recorder for the child to hear and repeat and then check his own errors.
   c. Using tactual and kinesthetic stimulation to help the child utilize the appropriate muscle groups.

2. Use choral reading and singing games.

3. Teach the child to blend sounds to form words (see Sound Blending).

4. Procure the advice of a speech correctionist or language pathologist in severe cases.

B. The child may lack adequate vocabulary

1. See suggestions for vocabulary development under Auditory Reception.

2. Teach the child to use his receptive vocabulary to express his ideas. Follow suggestions for imitation listed above and those under Section E for the child who lacks adequate interpersonal communication.

C. The child may not express ideas spontaneously (difficulty in retrieval of words or ideas)

1. The child who has difficulty retrieving the words he wishes to use can often be helped by:
    a. If the child has learned to imitate, prompting him, then asking questions. *Example:* "This is a ball. Say 'This is a ball.' " Then ask "What is this?" and require the answer "This is a ball" (see Bereiter and Engelmann, 1966).
    b. Providing a clue for the required word by giving the beginning sound and letting the child finish it (auditory closure). *Example:* "This is a sh— (shoe)." "I want a drink of wa—." "Where is my sis—?" Later say "I want a drink of w—." "Where is my s—?" Then let the child supply the whole word and immediately repeat the sentence without the clue.
    c. Providing a clue by showing a picture to stimulate retrieval of the required word; then gradually eliminate the use of pictures.
    d. If the child can read sentences, asking a question like "How old are you?" Then present the written sentence "I am six years old" for the child to read. Then repeat the question but do not show the sentence.
    e. Developing the habit of spontaneous recall by using words commonly associated together. Use auditory closure at the automatic level as a cue to stimulate meaningful closure. Have the child complete "Please pass the cream and ——." "The ball bounces up and ——." "It's raining cats and ——." "Here's the buttonhole; put in the ——." (If such combinations are not known, they may be taught through frequent exposure and repetition of opposites, common paired associates, and frequently associated ideas.)

2. For the child who has difficulty retrieving ideas, teach some strategies for retrieval by:

    a. Teaching the child to label objects, parts of the body, actions of himself or others. Use prompting, confirmation, and reinforcement.

    b. Teaching the child to take note of and describe his surroundings: (1) physical attributes of objects ("Tell me about this," i.e., color, size, texture, shape, smell, sound, taste), (2) functional attributes ("What is it used for?" "What does it do?"), (3) personal reaction to and association with it, (4) number and description of component parts.

    c. Developing in the child the ability to interpret pictures and experiences verbally.

D. The child may lack automatic grammatic skills

See Grammatic and Auditory Closure.

E. The child may lack adequate interpersonal communication

1. Prompt and reinforce the interchange of ideas through:

    a. Telephone conversations (real and imaginary).

    b. Taking turns telling parts of a story (one child starts where someone leaves off).

    c. Answering questions, supplying information.

    d. Developing sequences of ideas that are understandable to others, as in retelling stories, giving directions, relating experiences.

    e. Developing the ability to relate his own remarks to what others have said or are concerned about.

    f. Recording messages for other people on tape.

    g. Impersonating other persons or animals through dramatics, finger plays, puppetry, paper-doll play. Using masks or paper bags with faces drawn on them sometimes makes it easier for a child to identify with another character and speak for him. If the child does not speak spontaneously in free play, he may be helped to learn prescribed wordings and develop variations.

Grammatic and auditory closure (including sound blending)

Often a child is deficient in the ability to recognize and use common units of auditory experience when only parts of those units are presented. For such a child, remediation should be directed toward helping him automatically fill in the missing parts of what is partially heard. He must be helped to internalize certain redundancies from his experience. Some children learn these redundant units of experience more readily than others. These redundancies include common sequences of phonemes in words, the sequence of numerals in learning to count, sequences of sounds common in the particular language he hears, the order of words in a sentence, grammatic habits of inflecting words, and idioms of his particular language. They include, at least tangentially, the ability to synthesize isolated sounds into a word as in sound blending.

The ability to perform these various aspects of auditory closure should be evaluated separately and dealt with accordingly. The child's ability to develop adequate grammatic closure is of great importance because of its relationship to both auditory reception and verbal expression and therefore to its practical use in communicating with others and in acquiring academic skills.

In eliciting auditory closure, the likelihood that a specific response will be made is dependent upon such factors as: (a) the frequency and recency with which the child has heard the expression, (b) the number of alternatives possible, (c) the position in the expression of the parts omitted, (d) the number and length of the parts omitted, and (e) the order of approximation to English phonetic and syntactic structure.

The following guidelines are presented as suggestions for the teacher.

A. The child may not have had sufficient exposure to the material being presented

1. Select a few common expressions with which the child is not familiar and plan situations in which these expressions can be pre-

sented frequently in varying situations. As the child acquires these expressions, move on to others.

2. Rephrase the child's incorrect response incidentally. If he says "We writed a letter," you say "Yes, we *wrote* a letter. What did we do to the letter? We ——."

3. When necessary, point out differences between the desired response or usage and what the child has said.

4. If the child has difficulty learning to count from 1 to 10, perhaps he has not heard the customary sequence often enough. Provide situations in which he hears counting such as "one little, two little, three little Indians . . ." or some of the records and tapes which present counting experiences.

5. If it is desirable to teach the multiplication tables by rote, present repeated situations in which the child listens and repeats the sequences heard. There are records and tapes to familiarize the child with these routine facts.

6. Learning nursery rhymes often depends on repeated presentation of the same material. The frequency of presentation often determines the ease with which the child internalizes the expressions.

7. Present comparable visual material in juxtaposition to the auditory.

8. Provide motor experiences to give support to the auditory.

B. The child may lack adequate short-term auditory memory

See Auditory Sequential Memory.

C. The child may not reactivate what he hears, either vocally or subvocally

1. Have the child repeat what he hears. The teacher can make a statement and ask the child to repeat it: "We wrote a letter. What did we do?" There are many records and tapes in which the child responds either with the recorded voice or immediately after. A stereo tape can be used over and over, retaining the permanent material on one track and recording the child's responses temporarily on the other track.

2. Develop the habit of rehearsal. Have the child listen to material and say it to himself before he says it out loud.

3. Have the child hold material in mind long enough to select the same thing from multiple choices.

4. Use choral responses and group singing to give vocal experience and to trigger the correct response.

D. The child may not learn readily even when experiences have been repeated many times

1. Teach regular forms first. *Example:* Avoid irregular plurals and irregular verbs until the child has acquired a generalization of how to form regular plurals, how to indicate past tense, how to indicate ongoing action. In teaching regular past tense, use a singular noun such as "boy" consistently with verbs which use a regular past tense: "The boy played; the boy jumped; the boy climbed"; but *not* "The boy ran; the boy rode; the boy sang."

2. Later give repetitive exposure to the exceptions of language. Teach the irregular plurals and irregular verb forms through redundant experiences. Follow a sequential program.

3. In teaching syntax and word forms, develop a pattern for generating a particular form of expression and present verbal experiences following this pattern. Use model sentences to help teach the child to form new sentences which follow the same model. As he internalizes the correct pattern, move on to a new or expanded model. Use either a structural approach or a transformational approach by:

   a. With the structural approach, teaching the child the form of a simple identity sentence: "This is a pencil." Then supply incomplete sentences of similar form in which a particular word class (noun, verb, adjective, adverb) is missing and help the child repeat the whole sentence several times, each time adding a different word of the same class. *Example:* "This is a —— (cup, book, window, ring)." As he internalizes the correct pattern, choose more advanced material. *Example:* "The pencil is yellow." "The pencil is long and yellow." "The yellow pencil is long." "The pencils are yellow."

   b. With the transformational approach, supplying two sentences (or more) which can be transformed into one sentence through the processes of combining, substituting, and deleting. *Example:* "George is going to camp." "Jim is going to camp." These can be transformed into "George and Jim are going to camp." Or "This pencil is long," and "This pencil is yellow" can be transformed into "This yellow pencil is long," "This long pencil is yellow," or "This pencil is long and yellow."

4. Give extensive verbal practice to those forms you want the child to internalize. Have the child use the desired forms through imitation, choral reading, dramatics, and spontaneous speech.

5. Keep a checklist of the most common or most obvious errors the child makes and remediate these one at a time.

6. If the child has difficulty supplying the complete word from partial presentation, help him by:

   a. At first presenting the material to be used for closure in its completed form before asking the child to finish the incomplete form. *Example:* "I am going to say a word, 'potato.' Now you finish it, 'pota—.'"

   b. Next giving a clue but not the actual word he is to finish. *Example:* Use the partial word in a sentence or phrase to give a context clue. "Bread and bu—." "Daddy went to work. He went to the off—." "Write it on the black—."

   c. Then presenting familiar material in incomplete form. Ask the child to complete it without having heard it beforehand and without having been given clues. *Example:* "What word is this?" "Alliga—." "Wa—er." (This could be "Walter," "water," "walker," "washer," but not "waiter," "wafer," "waster.")

   d. Remembering the following factors in selecting words: (1) It is usually easier to supply the final sound or syllable; next easiest is the initial sound; most difficult is the internal sound, especially a whole syllable. (2) The words must be within the child's active expressive vocabulary. (3) It is more difficult if more than one part is eliminated, as in "wa—er—elon." (4) If the word is familiar to the child, a long word is easier than a short word because it gives him more clues.

E. The child may have difficulty synthesizing isolated sounds into words (sound blending)

1. One factor in the ease with which sounds can be blended into words is the rate at which they are presented. The closer they are presented in time, the more readily they will be blended.

a. If the child cannot blend sounds at a half-second interval, ask him to repeat the word after you, then to repeat it when you say it very slowly. *Example:* "What is this word: 'sh (half-second interval) oe'?" If the child cannot respond "Shoe," ask him to say "Shoe." Then, "What is this? Sh-sh-sh-oe-oe," with each sound prolonged but the two sounds running together. Then try another two-sound word like "m (half-second interval) ee."

b. When the child has learned to blend two sounds with a short interval between sounds, present the sounds at a slower and slower rate until he can synthesize them into a word when presented at two-second intervals. (The reason for teaching the child to blend sounds at a two-second interval is that later, when he uses a phonetic system in learning to read, a beginner requires two seconds to recognize a visual letter symbol and recall the sound associated with it. He must, then, hold one sound in mind for two seconds while he translates the next visual symbol into a sound. If the facility of blending sounds at a two-second interval has become automatic, he can then concentrate on recalling the sounds of phonemes rather than being faced with the dual task of recalling each phoneme while concentrating on blending successive sounds.)

2. Another factor in the ease with which sounds can be blended into words is the number of elements presented. The child can be aided here by:

a. Teaching him to blend words which have only two sounds as described above. Then proceed to three- and four-sound words.

b. Teaching him (after the child has achieved auditory synthesis for two-, three-, and four-sound words) to recognize visual symbols, "c-a-t," and blend their sounds into words. Phonic systems may differ in their approaches, but the prerequisite to all of them is adequate sound blending ability.

Auditory sequential memory

Some children have difficulty remembering what is heard long enough to repeat it immediately. Repeating meaningful sentences is easier than repeating such nonmeaningful sounds as digits, random words, or nonsense syllables. Remembering experiences or other material over a longer period of time, as in recalling a poem learned some time before, is considered long-term memory, whereas repeating digits just heard is considered short-term memory.

Children who have a deficiency in short-term auditory memory may also have difficulty in imitation of words and sentences. Learning to talk depends in part on the ability of a child to imitate words and sentences in his environment. Failure in this area may produce a child who is delayed in talking.

In training auditory memory it is advisable to use content that the child will utilize in his everyday life. For example, if a child does not talk or is delayed in talking and has a deficiency in auditory sequential memory, it is wise to train his auditory sequential memory with words, phrases, and sentences rather than with digits or nonsense syllables.

The following suggestions may be helpful in developing auditory sequential memory.

A. The child may have difficulty attending to details of auditory stimuli

1. See suggestions under Auditory Reception, Section B.

2. Help the child recognize the sequential nature of a pattern. Teach him to understand and use such words denoting position as "next to," "after," "before," "middle," "last," etc. Use these words to note the position of various parts of the sequence being learned.

3. Help direct attention to details, using motor cues, by:
   a. When presenting a series to be repeated by the child ("3-6-7," "c-a-t, h-o-u-s-e," or "apples-bananas-oranges"), tapping or making some dramatic gesture with each element of the series.

b. Asking the child to make some motor response such as tapping or clapping each time an item is given.

4. Help direct attention to details by using visual clues. Present visual clues momentarily along with the auditory stimulus but immediately remove the visual aid.

5. Use short periods demanding attention at first, providing reinforcement for attending. Then extend the time, using delayed or intermittent reinforcement.

6. Teach the child to discriminate small differences between pairs of sequences of words, letters, or tapes. *Example:* "Are these the same? 7-9-3, 7-3-9."

7. Ask the child to listen with his eyes closed.

**B. The child may have difficulty repeating
what he has heard and attended to**

1. Teach the child the following techniques (strategies) for immediate recall:
   a. Rehearsal. Teach the child to rehearse (repeat to himself) the first part of a stimulus while the rest is being presented.
   b. Grouping. Teach the child to group elements of a sequence in as large clusters as possible. *Example:* A telephone number is easier to remember as "237–87–01" than as "2378701."
   c. Visualization. Teach the child to integrate the sequence heard with a visual counterpart, visualizing the objects, letters, digits, or words. Or, if learning to repeat a rhythm of beats, integrate it with a visual presentation of dots and spaces or lines and spaces.
   d. Motor response. Teach the child to respond motorically as he hears the auditory stimulus. Imagining the motor response on a buzzer board as he hears the stimulus, or writing what he hears (even cursory writing in the air), may help some children.
   e. Making the stimulus meaningful, by using representational-level processes. Teach the child to repeat meaningful material since this is what he will use most often in everyday life. With arbitrary sequences such as room numbers and street addresses, help the child to note such relationships as

same beginning and end, double numbers, or quantitative sequences.

2. Two training methods which may be used are:
   a. Showing the child success by presenting sequences to be repeated that are within his range of possible accomplishment. Gradually increase the difficulty.
   b. Occasionally presenting tasks which are well beyond his ability to repeat on initial presentation. In this situation allow the child as many presentations as necessary to achieve success, but make it a game to see how few trials are necessary. If he can repeat three words fairly consistently, present sequences with four or five words and repeat until success is attained. This tends to stretch his ability.

3. In practical situations in which the child must utilize auditory sequential memory, use psychological principles to make recall easier by:
   a. Presenting the material at an optimum rate.
   b. Presenting sequences of an optimum length.
   c. If the syllables within the sequence are numerous, using fewer items in the sequence.
   d. Grouping the items to be repeated. A rhythmic presentation is easier to repeat than a monotonous one.
   e. Using visual and motor counterparts to the auditory presentation, as described above.

C. The child may have difficulty storing and retrieving information

1. Many of the strategies given under Sections A and B are applicable to memorizing or learning material for later recall (long-term memory).

2. Many of the techniques for developing auditory closure are applicable here.

3. Help the child use representational abilities and find identifiable characteristics and associations within material to be remembered. *Example:* The difference between "meet" and "meat" can be remembered because the one we eat has "eat" in it. Certain numbers begin and end with the same digit or have runs in them.

Visual reception

Some children find it difficult to translate visual symbols into meaning or to grasp the meaning of pictures. Remediation is directed toward helping these children to attach meaning to words and other written symbols and to interpret gestures, facial expressions, body posture, and pictorial representations and drawings of objects or actions.

Visual reception activities also involve functions at the automatic level. It is sometimes difficult to isolate behavior involving the representational level from that at the automatic level. Certainly it is necessary for the child to acquire adequate habits of visual-motor perception before he can derive meaning from what he sees. For this reason some of the following suggestions include activities to develop automatic-level abilities. Similarly, some of the suggestions involve activities demanding some visual association, for it is difficult to draw a sharp line between these two processes.

It is hoped that the following suggestions will be of some help in developing procedures for alleviating visual reception difficulties.

A. The child may lack prerequisite skills of visual-motor perception

1. Teach the child to recognize and differentiate various shapes and simple objects even when in different sizes, colors, and positions (form perception). Go beyond squares, circles, and triangles to faces, arrows, letters, and words.

2. Teach the child to recognize shapes when imbedded in other visual material (figure-ground perception). *Example:* Have him find the cup on a complex background, the letters on a block, the cat in the tree. Use hidden pictures, words, letters, and objects. Have him follow a line through a complex background or outline in different colors simple objects overlapping each other.

3. Teach the child to recognize and differentiate the position of objects in space: a chair in different positions, a face turned to the

right and left, the letters "b" and "d," and "p" and "q." Most readiness workbooks contain exercises to develop this ability.

4. Give the child experiences which will develop better body image and enable him to use his own body as a reference point to organize his visual environment (see Manual/Motor Expression).

5. Train the child to recognize the spatial relationship of objects to each other. Objects or pictures of objects and figures may be above, below, beside each other, back in the distance (smaller) or close up (larger), or one behind the other. Motor experience is important here. Have the child connect dots, copy figures and letters, complete common shapes, put together simple jigsaw puzzles, walk the distance or feel the distance between various objects.

6. Develop adequate eye-hand and eye-body coordination (see Manual/Motor Expression).

7. Develop the ability to perceive more rapidly (speed of perception) (see Visual Closure).

8. See Frostig and Horne (1964), Kephart (1960), and Getman *et al.* (1968).

B. The child may lack knowledge and experience

1. Allow the child active participation with such things in his environment as household objects, manipulative toys, school materials, common foods, colors, letters.

2. Provide experiences in shopping, traveling, visiting places and people of interest, and organized field trips.

3. Label and discuss what he sees and how things function. *Example:* "A bus takes people places." "Sewing holds things together." "A saw cuts wood."

4. Read appropriate stories and use films which expand the child's knowledge of his environment.

C. The child may not observe things within his visual field

1. Train the child to note and talk about what he sees. Play games to see who can note the most objects in a store window or on the teacher's desk.

2. Train the child to look at things as if he must remember what he

saw. Play detective games in which the child is allowed a limited time to note things in his environment. *Example:* Bring him into a room where there are three or four people doing different things and certain objects lying around, or arrange similar activities in a doll house. Then take him out and ask him to name who was there, what they were doing, what was on the table, who was sitting down (see Visual Sequential Memory).

3. Teach the child to note and describe various attributes of objects. *Example:* "A book has a soft cover (or a hard cover); it is thin or thick; it is red (or ——); it has lots of (or few) pages" (see Verbal Expression).

4. Play guessing games in which the child identifies objects by their description (see Auditory Reception).

D. The child may not attach meaning to visual symbols

1. Teach the child to gain meaning from symbols and pictures by:
   a. Helping the child recognize and discriminate color, size, shape, pictures of people, of foods, of furniture, clothing, toys.
   b. Utilizing field trips and other experiences to apply meaning to pictorial representations. Take snapshots. Have the child find pertinent pictures. Have him sort pictures that do and do not represent the experience.
   c. Using stories to associate with pictures: (1) Discuss the illustrations, label contents, describe them. (2) Let the child find or draw pictures to illustrate stories. (3) Use stories with double meaning so that the child must understand the picture to understand the story. (4) Begin a story and finish with pictures. Have the child verbalize from the pictures. Or have him complete the story by selecting pictures.
   d. Letting the child make up stories about pictures or explain pictures to a younger child.
   e. Letting the child verbalize what he sees.
   f. Letting the child match his actions to pictures or select pictures to match actions.
   g. Finding (if a child has difficulty identifying objects in pictures) more realistic colored pictures which are counterparts of real (matching) objects. Using operant conditioning, reinforce the child when he selects the appropriate picture. Then follow

the same procedure for black and white reproductions, then outline drawings, then silhouettes.

h. Having the child make shadow pictures by drawing around the shadows of objects cast by a bright light onto newsprint hanging on the wall. Make profiles of people, shapes of hands.

2. Teach the child to gain meaning from arrows, traffic lights, stop signs, symbols for cross roads, curving highways, railroad crossings. These are symbols and must be associated with their appropriate concepts and verbal descriptions.

3. Teach the child to gain meaning from gestures and facial expressions (coordinate with Manual/Motor Expression) by:

a. Teaching the child to understand such common gestures as "Come here," "Go away," "Keep quiet," "Bye-bye," "Come in," "Yes," "No," "I don't know," "Good luck," scolding, threatening.

b. Playing "Let's pretend" games of household and school activities, sharpening a pencil, playing a piano, riding a horse, etc. The important aspect here is how well the child can interpret what other children are doing.

c. Pantomiming consecutive activities: (1) sawing a board, hammering a nail in, hitting your finger; or (2) writing a letter, folding it, putting it in an envelope, licking the flap, addressing it, putting on a stamp. Have the child explain the activity verbally.

d. Helping the child interpret facial expressions: surprise, disappointment, amusement, anger.

4. Develop in the child the ability to gain meaning from maps and diagrams by:

a. Helping the child follow diagrams for putting together simple paper and cardboard objects provided on cereal boxes, paper-folding activities, and dimestore construction kits. Put together model cars and airplanes from the picture directions.

b. Having him walk around the room and record his footsteps and objects he touches. Then use the same pattern for drawing a map. Extend this to larger areas. Have the child identify such "maps" by their individual characteristics.

5. Teach the child to gain meaning from printed letters and words.

Teach reading by a systematic method applicable to the child. Basically, children come to school with an understanding of auditory symbols (words and phrases). They must learn visual symbols comparable to the auditory symbols they already know. Learning to read, then, is the process of learning to gain meaning from visually presented symbols. In teaching reading the teacher includes visual discrimination, visual recognition of letters and words, and ultimately the meaning of complex visual symbols. Various methods of teaching reading may differ in their modes of presentation ("look and say," phonic, or linguistic methods), but all are striving for the goal of meaningful interpretation of the printed symbol.

6. Teach the child to gain meaning from arithmetic symbols by:
   a. Teaching the child to visually recognize one-ness, two-ness, three-ness, and four-ness. He may have to use enumeration at first but can learn to identify them at a glance through experience (tachistoscope, dominoes, and other games requiring increasingly rapid recognition).
   b. Teaching the child to attach meaning to the visual symbols of quantity. *Example:* The numeral "3" means (1) three-ness, (2) the label "three," and (3) the quantity between 2 and 4.
   c. Strengthening the associations between the verbal label and the visual symbol. Use motor-kinesthetic activity, tapping out the number, feeling the shape of the numeral, and writing the numerals as he speaks the label. If motor coordination is poor, the child can use a stylus in a block that has the numerals indented or cut into it. Felt numerals or three-dimensional numerals can also be used as a preliminary or collateral adjunct to learning to identify written numerals.

E. The child may not utilize visual imagery

1. Develop memory for things seen earlier by:
   a. Having the child describe what he remembers having seen: places he has been, people he has seen, colors of clothing, location of furniture.
   b. Having the child draw what he has seen.
   c. Having the child move (blindfolded) among obstacles in a room he has been allowed to observe.

2. Develop the ability to translate other sense impressions into visual images by:
   a. Having the child feel an object, then select the picture of it from several choices.
   b. Showing the child an object, then having him find it blindfolded among several other objects in a box or bag.
   c. Tapping out a rhythm and having the child draw or select from optional drawings the appropriate one: "II   II   II," "I   II   I," or "I   III."
   d. Describing the details of an object or a scene and having the child draw it or select the appropriate picture.

3. Develop the ability to create visual images by:
   a. Playing "Let's imagine." Can the child imagine a train with wings? Have him draw it. Can he imagine a man with two heads? A man who is fatter than he is tall? A green sky and blue grass? A bird with four legs? A cup with three handles?
   b. Playing imaginary "Hide the thimble." With eyes closed, imagine where to hide the thimble. The other person tells where he is looking for the thimble.
   c. Having the child look at a word, then close his eyes and try to think what it looked like. If he cannot develop an image of it, he should open his eyes and look again. Repeat until he thinks he can see it in his "mind's eye." This involves a sequence of letters and short-term memory (see Visual Sequential Memory).

Visual association

The process of association has been discussed on p. 143 under Auditory Association. With this rationale in mind, the following suggestions may help the teacher find and develop materials and activities to help the child derive understanding of visual relationships.

A. The child may have difficulty holding two or more concepts in mind and considering them in relation to each other

1. Teach the child to make comparisons between two pictures, two words, or two objects and to shift from one to the other. Verbalize the salient points of each. *Example:* "Here is a boy and here is a boy. This boy is fishing and this boy is playing baseball. This boy is standing up and this boy is sitting down. This boy is having fun and this boy is having fun. This boy has a hat on and this boy has a hat on. Which boy has a hat on? Does the other boy have a hat on? Do they *both* have hats on? Are they *both* having fun? What are they doing that is different?"

2. Have the child verbalize and point to comparable parts of an object and its picture. Have him describe each. Ask him leading questions. Give him verbal and graphic clues.

3. Ask the child to find pictures or objects that satisfy *two* requirements: something that is both soft *and* heavy, small *and* sharp, or hard *and* round.

4. Provide situations in which the child responds only when two objects have a specified relationship. *Example:* Using two cards, have the child respond only when both are the same color, or both show something to eat, or when one is bigger than the other. Some card games such as Snap and Flinch require this. Similar homemade games can be devised.

5. Demonstrate Piaget-type tasks of conservation and help the child focus on more than one dimension. *Example:* Using equal

balls of plasticine, flatten one out and call attention to both width *and* height of the pieces, one being wider and the other higher. Even if the child does not grasp the concept of conservation of mass, he can learn to evaluate the pieces in more than one dimension.

6. Workbooks and remedial exercises contain a large variety of activities which exemplify this requirement. In finding the bat that goes with the ball or the bird that goes with the airplane, the child has to hold two concepts in mind.

B. The child may have difficulty identifying first-order relationships (directly relating two visual concepts)

1. Help the child learn to identify opposite concepts presented in visual form by:
   a. Beginning with tangible characteristics: big-little, white-black, up-down, straight-crooked, right-left (i.e., this way–that way), square-round, full-empty, rough-smooth.
   b. Progressing to more abstract ideas which may have to be verbalized: happy-sad, fast-slow, like-dislike, good-bad.

2. Help the child learn to identify similarities and differences between pictures, letters, street signs, words, designs, and abstract ideas presented in pictorial form by:
   a. Beginning with examples which have obvious relationships and progressing to more subtle differences.
   b. Using tangible similarities first (such as analogous parts or comparable shape, size, color). Then incorporate less concrete relationships such as use, origin, class to which they belong (see Section D, 2).
   c. Remembering that (other things being equal) it is easier for a child to note differences than similarities if the pictures are comparable. It is easier to find the difference between a fish and a dog than to note how a fish and a dog are alike.
   d. Having the child mark comparable parts of pictures.
   e. Having the child verbalize similarities and differences.
   f. Having the child match pictures and explain why. Provide clusters of pictures with two things flying, two things swimming, two foods, two square things. Have him pick out ones that belong together and also explain wherein they are different.

g. Helping the child find missing parts in a picture (this also involves visual perception).

3. Help the child derive relationships other than analogous parts, functions, appearance. Help him see relationships of parts to whole (doorknob to a door, leaf to a tree), things commonly seen together (salt and pepper, cream and sugar, cup and saucer), things used together to perform a certain function (hammer and nails, pencil and paper, button and buttonhole), tool and user (painter and paintbrush, foot and shoe).

4. Help the child derive cause-and-effect relationships by:
   a. Showing the child a picture of boys playing ball near a window (the child selects the next picture with a broken or unbroken window); or of a child running and about to stumble on a big rock (the child selects the appropriate picture to follow).
   b. Helping him verbalize such relationships in relation to the pictures.
   c. Having the child draw or select from alternatives what a capped jar of liquid would look like if tipped in different positions; or what would happen if one block in a tower of blocks is moved (tower would lean, tower would hold, tower would fall, tower would shrink, etc.).

5. Help the child derive time and space relationships by:
   a. Helping the child relate time to quantity. "Watch the pile of sand grow larger in an hour glass or three-minute timer as time passes." "Pile one block every second and see how the tower grows." "Save one nickel every day and see how the money grows."
   b. Helping the child relate time to space. Note the changing position of the sun as time passes. Note the movement of the hands on the clock. "Which letter in a word is sounded first?" "Which letter in your name do you write first?"
   c. Helping the child relate time to visual representations of the environment: summer and winter, day and night, sequence of holidays.
   d. Helping the child relate time to action. (1) Note the time it takes to walk across the room slowly and the time it takes to walk the same distance quickly. (2) Note the passage of time while holding one's breath. Or play Statuary to see how

long one position can be held. (3) Show "before" and "after" pictures of falling in the mud, getting in a fight, getting dressed in the morning, painting a house. (4) Show sequences of activities and have the child put picture sequences in the right order: sequence of activities during the day; or preparing dinner, eating dinner, and washing dishes; or getting a glass, pouring milk, and drinking it.

e. Teaching the child to synchronize action with a moving body. *Example:* Suspend a soft rubber ball to swing as a pendulum and have the child touch it just as it passes him. Or have him drop a pebble in a cup that is rotating on the edge of a disc.

f. Helping the child relate time to the calendar and the clock. Demonstrate yesterday, today, and tomorrow with pictures of experiences the child has had. Represent the days of the week by specific activities in school. Relate the position of the hands of the clock by certain activities.

6. Help the child derive number and space relationships by:

a. Developing an understanding of the point-to-point correspondence between number of objects and numerical symbols, utilizing haptic-kinesthetic and tactual as well as verbal counterparts.

b. Associating number sequences with their quantitative equivalents. *Example:* The quantity represented by the numeral "3" is one more than that represented by "2" and one less than that represented by "4."

c. Using verbal and visual experiences to help the child understand the relationships of parts to the whole (combinations such as $3 + 1 = 4$) and parts to parts ($2 + 2 = 3 + 1$).

d. Providing many experiences to show number relations, as most arithmetic workbooks do. These should be integrated with the child's verbal understanding as well as his ability to relate visual counterparts.

C. The child may have difficulty identifying second-order relationships (finding a specific relationship to match one already given)

1. Help the child derive a specific relationship between two visual representations, a relationship which is exemplified by another pair of pictures. The child must take two steps; help him by:

a. Having him identify what kind of relationship exists in a particular picture or between two visual representations. *Exam-*

ple: The child can be helped to see the relationships of functions or actions in each of the following pictures: (1) a basketball player throwing a basketball; (2) a baseball player throwing a baseball; (3) a baseball player batting a ball; (4) a tennis player hitting a ball. Each of these would be considered a first-order relationship.

  b. To help the child find a second-order relationship, giving him one of the above-mentioned pictures and asking him to find a comparable picture from the other three.

2. Pictorial analogies require the child to find these second-order relationships. *Example:* The child might be shown a picture of a dog and one of a bone, then helped to find the appropriate picture to go with a cat: a mouse or a bowl of milk.

D. The child may have difficulty classifying or categorizing visual concepts

1. Demonstrate and help the child classify concepts into "sets" by:
  a. Helping the child find pictures or objects that fit specified categories, beginning with a single class.
  b. Demonstrating and helping the child select pictures which *do not* fit a selected group of pictures.
  c. Defining verbally when there is any doubt as to what a particular category includes and does not include. Ask the child to explain verbally how things are related and why he places certain pictures together.
  d. Teaching the child to devise his own categories for a series of pictures presented to him: a cat, a dog, a chair, a horse, a stove, a bed.
  e. Teaching the child that there may be several ways to classify the same objects. *Example:* Triangles, circles, and squares of different colors may be sorted according to shape or color.
  f. Teaching the child ways of finding common elements among objects or pictures to be categorized. *Example:* "Is their structure similar (wheels, steps, shape, layers, etc.)? Are they used in a similar manner or for a similar purpose? Is their shape, color, size, texture similar? Are they of the same composition?" The child should be taught to be flexible and examine these various elements of commonality.

2. Demonstrate and help the child to understand "subsets" by:
  a. Letting him select pictures which represent a certain cate-

gory, then subdivide these pictures according to subcategories. Foods could be subdivided into solids and liquids, fruits, vegetables, meat. Help him understand that there are categories within categories.
  b. Demonstrating that a hen is a chicken but a chicken is not always a hen; a dog is an animal but not all animals are dogs; a subset fits into a set but a set does not fit into a subset.

**E. The child may have difficulty finding
and evaluating alternative solutions to a problem**

1. Develop ideational fluency in order to help the child see more possibilities for relationships and solutions by:
  a. Brainstorming. Find as many different meanings, as many attributes, as many relationships, as many associated visual images for a picture as possible. This should not be done idly but directed toward the goal of finding a solution to a problem.
  b. Accepting divergent responses with respect. They can be evaluated later.
  c. In arranging pictures or sequences of figures, encouraging the child to try many different possibilities. Some materials lend themselves to this more than others. *Example:* A series of pictures depicting a story sequence might have to be rearranged several times to find a logical sequence.
  d. Presenting an incomplete set of pictures with a variety of alternatives to complete it, some possible, some impossible, and some better than others.
  e. Reading a story and having the child illustrate it. He can draw pictures or cut them from magazines, providing a variety of interpretations.
  f. Presenting pictures which have had some item in the picture cut out (like the Healy Picture Completion Tests), all pieces cut out the same shape. Give the child a supply of other pictures cut out in the same shape and size and ask him to find the best picture for each empty space. The items removed should all be meaningful but more and less relevant.

2. Increase flexibility in thinking by:
  a. Developing the ability to cross from one modality to another.

Associate pictures with words, sentences, and stories. Translate words into movement, rhythm, or pictures and vice versa.

  b. Developing the ability to take a new look at a problem or situation. If one approach does not work, try a new approach. If, in categorizing objects, the child is thinking only of physical attributes, suggest action, or function, or place of origin (from trees, from sheep, from the ground).

  c. Developing empathy for other individuals or for characters in a story. Ask the child to see a scene as it would look to someone sitting on the other side of the room. *Example:* Present a series of drawings or pictures of things on the teacher's desk seen from different angles and positions. Have the child select the view as seen from the side of the desk, the end of the desk.

3. Develop evaluative thinking or the ability to "find the match" by:

  a. Helping the child learn to specify the problem or goal. If he is finding a picture to complete a story, what problem must be solved? What has gone before? What facts does he know? If he is finding a picture that matches a word, what are the characteristics required? State the problem.

  b. Selecting the various possibilities and evaluating the results of using each.

  c. Finding not *a* solution but the *best* solution.

  d. Teaching the child to guess, then test his guess.

  e. Helping the child note the incongruities in picture absurdities: ice skating on the sidewalk, walking down the street with one shoe off, an airplane without wings, eating soup with the spoon upside down.

Manual/motor expression

Remediation in this area aims to increase a child's ability to express his ideas in nonverbal, motor terms. Some deaf children learn finger spelling or the manual language and are able to express their ideas by use of their fingers or hands. This is one form of manual expression. There are various reasons that a child fails to develop this ability. Sometimes he lacks the basic bodily orientation to make such activity meaningful. Sometimes he lacks the ability to express an idea in nonverbal terms. Sometimes his cultural and experiential background has not stimulated this kind of communication. He therefore is apt to find it difficult to draw, write, gesticulate, or demonstrate manual operations. This often hinders academic progress.

Some suggestions are presented here which may help develop this ability.

A. The child may lack prerequisite perceptual-motor skills

1. Develop adequate body image: posture and balance, spatial awareness, bodily orientation in relation to other people and objects, identification of body parts, left-right orientation, ability to repeat movements of others (see Kephart, 1960).

2. Develop *prerequisite* skills of visual-motor perception (see suggestions under Visual Reception).

3. Develop ocular control: the ability to follow a moving object, to shift the eye fixation, to keep the eyes on an object for an extended period (see Getman *et al.,* 1968; Kephart, 1960).

4. Develop gross motor control: hopping, skipping, jumping, catching and throwing a ball, turning a crank, following a rhythm, and keeping time.

5. Develop eye-hand coordination: tracing, following the dots, continuing an unfinished line, drawing parallel lines (see Frostig and Horne, 1964, and exercises in many readiness workbooks).

175

6. Develop fine motor coordination: scribbling, fingerpainting, clay-modeling, paper-folding, cutting, turning a small knob or screwing a lid on a jar, buttoning and unbuttoning, drawing a circle, activating specific body parts on command (verbal or gestural), copying simple forms, letters, and numbers.

B. The child may lack ideas leading to motor expression

1. Demonstrate the kinds of ideas that can be expressed motorically:
   a. Actions: fighting, sleeping, running, driving a car, riding a horse, hammering a nail, digging a hole.
   b. Emotions: fear, joy, anger, determination, dislike, resignation.
   c. Occupations and personalities: schoolteacher, cross parent, orator, carpenter, painter.
   d. Physical qualities: size, shape, number, weight.
   e. Directions: right, left, up, down, over there, straight ahead, back there.
   f. Common gestures: "Come here," "Shh," "Go away," "Stop," "Bye-bye," "Yes," "No," "I don't know."

2. Develop imagination or make-believe by:
   a. Dramatizing stories.
   b. Acting out songs.
   c. Expressing rhythms and feelings derived from music: fast, slow, twirling, jumping, happy, sad, angry.
   d. Helping the child identify with some character or animal in a story. Talk about how he feels and what he would do, then act it out. Use actual props first if necessary; then go through movements without props.
   e. Imitating inanimate objects: a tree, a ball, a jumping jack.

C. The child may not make ideas operational

1. Provide motor activities in which a product is involved: sandbox activities, clay-modeling, paper-folding, drawing and painting, writing, using codes.

2. Provide transitory motor-expressive activities: charades, pantomimes, and tableaux; dramatizing stories with or without verbal involvement, but using as much gesture as possible; finger plays; dance; gestural conversation; nonverbal Password.

Visual closure

Remediating a visual closure deficit involves giving the child those experiences which help him to organize and integrate his visual field automatically to create a recognizable visual percept. This may involve the ability to fill in missing parts automatically. It may involve extracting the necessary parts from a distracting background. It may involve rejecting extraneous superimposed marks such as the cross-hatching effect of a screen, a fence, a blot of ink, or a smear of mud. It may involve selecting the relevant parts from a visual field that includes irrelevant pieces or altering parts of the visual field to fit a visual image as in the Rorschach. Or it may involve reorienting the pieces and putting them together as in the object assembly test of the WISC. Many workbooks and readiness activities for children include a combination of these activities.

Reading itself includes visual closure, since with each fixation of the eye only part of the letters of a word or phrase are actually perceived. Observations of eye movements during reading indicate that an average reader in the fourth or fifth grade has three or four fixations per line whereas an average reader in the first grade has eight to twelve fixations. As a reader becomes more competent, his eye fixations become fewer, and with fewer fixations he must fill in more material and encompass a wider area of the printed matter. Some of this, of course, is meaningful closure whereby the reader "closes" an idea rather than a visual percept.

It may well be that during the process of learning to read the child develops visual closure and speed of perception. Reading itself may be a good experience for developing closure. Whenever possible, visual closure activities should be developed around letters, words, and phrases, since this is the most important school task to which visual closure is applicable. For the younger child, other forms of visual closure may be necessary as a preliminary experience to bringing closure to bear on reading material.

Some of the following suggestions may be applicable to developing visual closure.

A. The child may lack prerequisite perceptual-motor skills

See Visual Reception, Section A, particularly 1 and 2.

B. The child may lack the ability to visualize

1. See Visual Reception, Section E.

2. Present a visual stimulus (word, letter, picture, color patch) for a few seconds and then have the child select the same item from multiple choices (two or three alternatives at first, then more choices as he improves). Lengthen or repeat the initial presentation as needed.

3. Provide a similar presentation with a delayed response.

4. Provide a similar task, asking the child to visualize from a verbal instead of a visual stimulus.

5. Provide a similar presentation using incomplete pictures for the choices but complete pictures for the stimulus and vice versa.

6. Provide a similar presentation using imbedded and/or mutilated figures.

C. The child may lack the ability to organize a disparate visual field into a unified percept

1. Present closure experiences in which the child must integrate all parts presented by:
    a. Using a stereopticon to demonstrate how parts combine to make a recognizable whole. *Example:* Put a bird cage on the card for one eye and a bird on the card for the other eye (through fusion, the bird will appear to be in the cage). Or put part of the child's name on one card and the rest of it on the other. Or do the same with parts of digits or faces. Then show the child disparate parts and help him integrate them without the stereopticon.
    b. Letting the child put together commercial formboards and jigsaw puzzles of gradually increasing difficulty, with and without seeing the completed model. Use simple human figures clearly differentiated from the background at first. Make the total picture more interesting than the pieces.
    c. Having the child approach the task analytically as well as synthetically. Have him take apart a model such as a card-

board manikin clipped together at the joints and then put it together again. Or have him make his own jigsaw puzzles, using enlarged photographs of himself and classmates. Or have him cut up his own name and other words or phrases he knows.

    d. Using anagrams to develop visual closure for common words.

    e. Instead of using movable pieces, distributing parts of a word or picture on a page and having the child select the correct closure from alternative choices. Later have him supply the answer from an open-ended field. In the beginning have the parts in proper orientation and attitude. When necessary, diminish the gap between the parts until the child can "see" the closure of disparate parts. Increase the difficulty by (1) using more pieces, (2) placing them farther apart, and (3) changing the attitude and orientation.

2. Present experiences in which some parts are missing such as:

    a. Having the child identify incomplete pictures and words by labeling or finding the completed model or by drawing it. (1) If the child does not achieve closure, provide a series of possible models from which he can find the match. (2) If he still has difficulty with closure, put the incomplete figure on onionskin paper and have him superimpose it on the possible models. (3) Give additional clues where necessary by supplying additional parts of the unfinished figure or using verbal clues to call attention to existing parts of the incomplete figure. *Example:* With an incomplete coffeepot, ask what he thinks the handle is (have him label it). "Could it be a cup? A tool? A wagon? A pitcher? A coffeepot?" (4) Prepare a guessing game in which the child is presented with a series of cards, each successive card having more clues (more completed) than the preceding one. The score depends on how many cards the child must look at before he can guess correctly. If the child jumps the gun and guesses wildly, introduce a penalty for wrong answers. Or pictures and words can be covered and gradually exposed to see how soon they can be identified.

    b. Providing a series of out-of-focus pictures in which each successive picture is more clearly in focus than the preceding one. Score according to the number of pictures needed to identify the picture or words.

c. Having the child identify silhouettes and outline figures which lack detail.

d. Having the child identify dotted outlines. Connect the dots if necessary. If he can identify numbers, have him connect dots according to number.

e. Having the child identify pictures with cracks in them or pictures on crumpled paper (then flatten them out).

f. Having the child identify pictures and words seen through various thicknesses of wire mesh or tissue; or superimpose a fence or hatch marks over the picture.

3. Present experiences in which the child must extract a word or figure which is partially imbedded in another figure by:

a. Having the child trace around figures or color the letters in a word that is superimposed on a distracting background.

b. Having the child play detective and decipher a map or message written on top of a picture.

4. Present experiences in which some parts are not used such as:

a. Cutting common shapes into jigsaw puzzles but including an extra piece.

b. Mixing the pieces of two jigsaw puzzles together. Simplify by cutting two pictures (i.e., an apple and an orange) each in half and have the child put them together.

D. The child may lack adequate speed of perception

1. Use a tachistoscopic presentation of words and pictures to develop speed of perception by:

a. Having the child label or point to its counterpart as soon as recognized.

b. Gradually decreasing the time of exposure.

c. Developing rapid recognition by limiting the number and similarity of pictures. Then add new items and more similar ones as the child recognizes the original pictures readily. *Example:* The child has been shown a ball, a hammer, and a ladder-back chair; these are presented in random order on the tachistoscope, gradually reducing the time of exposure. When the child becomes facile in identifying these, add more objects and similar objects: an apple, a walking stick (cane), and a ladder.

2. Play such card games as Snap and Flinch which require rapid recognition of the stimulus.

Visual sequential memory

Remediation of a deficit in visual sequential memory is directed toward helping the child perceive and remember a sequence of objects, letters, words, or other symbols in the same order as originally seen. This ability is of vital importance in learning to read and spell. Studies cited in Chapter 3 indicate that retarded readers have poorer visual sequential memory than children with similar intelligence who are good readers.

Some children are able to remember and reproduce a design or form but are unable to remember and reproduce a series of symbols in the sequence presented. It is the latter kind of visual memory that seems to be related to reading.

How much of sequential memory ability is organismically determined is difficult to say. Undoubtedly, there are other factors affecting success in this area. Experience, motivation, maturation, and ability to concentrate probably enter in. Awareness of details and of the sequential nature of the task are probably factors.

Basic perceptual skills, especially if based on central or peripheral visual defects, influence the ability to "see" the sequence accurately. A child with fusion difficulty or with distorted body orientation, for instance, may perceive "saw" as "was" or "no" as "on." Children with eye-muscle imbalance may have difficulty in that they see the same word differently at different times. When the eye muscles are fatigued, the child gains a different impression of the word than he does when fresh and able to give greater concentration to the control of his vision. Reading itself, according to some ophthalmologists, is good orthoptic training and may be the most helpful activity for a child with even slight eye-muscle difficulty.

For the child who does not respond well to repeated efforts to improve visual short-term memory, some strategies may be necessary to provide the functional ability to remember the sequences necessary to spell and read.

Some suggestions which may be helpful are given in the following pages.

A. The child may show physical correlates inhibiting development of visual sequential memory

1. If the child's behavior indicates it, refer him to an ophthalmologist for specific determination of the phorias, accommodation, convergence, and other anomalies which may inhibit accurate perception and visual fusion.

2. Adapt instruction to any visual anomaly or orientation difficulty by giving short periods of concentrated effort to achieve perception and fusion.

3. Use motor responses of the child to improve orientation.

4. Help the child develop visual-motor perceptual abilities (see Visual Reception, Section A).

B. The child may have difficulty attending to visual details

1. Arrange instructional materials in such a way as to emphasize attention to details by:
   a. Underlining certain letter combinations or using color to call attention to parts often ignored.
   b. Increasing the time of attention gradually.

2. Develop attention to details through games, surprises, and social or tangible reinforcers.

3. Develop ability to note details by showing objects or pictures, then removing one or two to see if the child can remember which one is missing; or, when the piece is removed, have him select it from a group of items, the rest of which are not used.

C. The child may have difficulty remembering what he has seen and attended to

1. Help the child recognize the sequential nature of patterns, i.e., that there is a particular order. Show him a sequence in an order that he knows, such as small, medium, and large blocks or dominoes with one, two, and three spots, and ask him to repeat it. Or use a face cut into three cross-wise strips. Have the child reproduce the logical sequence first; then reverse it; then put the parts in an illogical sequence to be reproduced.

2. Have the child copy the pattern first, if necessary, without removal of the model. Then have him copy it with the model hidden, but give him the privilege of peeking when he cannot remember. Gradually remove this privilege.

3. Two training methods which may be used are:
   a. Showing the child success by presenting sequences to be reproduced that are within his range of possible accomplishment. Gradually increase the difficulty.
   b. Occasionally presenting tasks which are well beyond his ability to reproduce on initial presentation. In this situation allow the child as many presentations as necessary to achieve success, but make it a game to see how few trials are necessary. If he can reproduce two symbols fairly consistently, present sequences with four or five symbols and repeat until success is achieved. This tends to stretch his ability.

4. Teach the child some techniques (strategies) for immediate recall:
   a. Rehearsal. Teach the child to rapidly review what he has seen before, trying to reproduce it. "Look at it; then close your eyes and rehearse it; then look back at the model to check your image."
   b. Grouping. Teach the child to break down the sequence into segments such as the first two or three and the last two or three elements. Or find patterns such as alternate figures or first and last figures being the same.
   c. Verbalization. Let the child verbalize the sequence. Show the child a sequence of objects, pictures, letters, or words; then cover them and have the child label them in order. If successful, confirm by showing him the objects again; if unsuccessful, show the objects and have him try again.
   d. Motor response. Have the child copy the sequence, or, if pictures are used, demonstrate the action.
   e. Making the stimulus meaningful by using representational-level processes. Use purposeful material rather than irrelevant sequences. With arbitrary sequences such as room numbers, street addresses, or zip codes, teach the child to find logical relationships: numbers going from large to small or small to large, or the same beginning and end, or alternating sequences.

5. Use a variety of materials and situations: bead-stringing, copying a sequence of bodily movements (touching knees, head, shoulder; clapping hands; jumping; bending), replacing objects on a desk or the chalkboard, reproducing numbers or letters, using anagrams to reproduce words, identifying misspelled words, finger plays, copying on pegboard sequences from memory. Learning to reproduce letter sequences (spelling) or words (reading) is most effective for the older child. For younger children, many activities can be patterned after spelling and reading in simplified form.

**D. The child may be unable to read and spell
due to a visual sequential memory deficit**

1. Give the child familiarity with letters and words, using the same procedures as was used with objects and pictures listed above.

2. Teach the child to reproduce from memory and in writing (if the child can write) words that will be used in reading and spelling. An adaptation of the Fernald kinesthetic method has been shown to increase visual sequential memory. This may be done by:

  a. Presenting the child with a word he does not know, labeling it for him, and having him say it. Then cover the word and ask him to reproduce it in writing. Then uncover the word and teach the child to monitor his own production. If correct, go on to another word. If unsuccessful, cover it and have the child try again.

  b. Increasing the length of the words as the child learns.

  c. When the child has acquired a vocabulary, using phrases and sentences within his ability to reproduce them in two to three trials.

  d. If the child has been trained in phonics, using nonphonic words like "though," "through," or "listen" to focus attention on visualization.

  e. To emphasize visualization, having the child look at the word. Trace it in the air, then write it and say it.

  f. Keeping in mind that the motor response of vocalizing and the feedback of kinesthesis as he writes aids the ability to visualize.

**E. The child may have difficulty storing
and retrieving information once learned**

Initiate training by overlearning the words presented. This may be accomplished by teaching one word, then another, then back to the first word, then the second. When teaching a third word, return to the first and second words learned. Overlearning counteracts retroactive inhibition. Use reinforcements for learning and writing words from memory and recalling them later. Ordinarily social reinforcement and success experience, with confirmation after the child's correct response, are sufficient. If not, for very hyperactive or negativistic children, use tangible reinforcement. Relearn words learned the previous day before going on to new words.

Concluding remarks

In utilizing the concepts presented here there is no substitute for a thorough understanding of the model of communication presented in Chapters 2 and 7. The remedial teacher must understand the disabilities of the child she is helping before she can devise a program of remediation. It is through this understanding that she can utilize the feedback she receives from the child to provide the ongoing diagnosis which is so important in remediation.

Remediation for children with specific learning disabilities is not promoted best by routine lesson plans prepared for a broad spectrum of children. There are on the market today many materials and step-by-step methods purportedly for "children with learning disabilities." Some of these are visual discrimination exercises, some are for motor development, etc. For particular children these may be very useful, but no one method is applicable to all children with learning disabilities.

There are many workbooks, commercial materials, and suggested activities that will give the teacher suggestions for the remediation of disabilities in a child. The remedial teacher's responsibility is to select the appropriate materials and activities. Remedial teaching requires not blindly using a particular workbook or method but, rather, understanding the goal to be achieved and finding appropriate means of attaining it. No attempt will be made here to list instructional materials, since these are quite extensive and can be obtained from commercial companies and from the numerous instructional materials centers.

In selecting a procedure or materials the remedial teacher will find valuable suggestions from the numerous books and activities for children. These materials may not be labeled (or may be mislabeled) as for auditory association, or motor expression, or auditory closure. It is the responsibility of the teacher to ask, "What does this material do?" or "What functions are required to accomplish this task?" Regardless of its label or its claim, the material should be analyzed by the remedial teacher to determine whether or not it is suitable for the particular problem she is trying to ameliorate. If not, she may have to change or adapt it to the needs of that particular child. For example, the activity of "show and tell" which is frequently used in the kindergarten and primary grades requests children to bring something to school which they can tell the class about. This common exercise is usually used to stimulate verbal expression but can be adapted to emphasize other functions. Each activity used by the teacher should be used after the remedial teacher has answered the question, "What specifically does this method, activity, or material develop in the child?"

Although no effort is made here to present an extensive list of remedial materials, the following references are given because the content was developed or stimulated by the model of the ITPA.

Karnes, M. B., *et al. Activities for developing psycholinguistic skills with preschool culturally disadvantaged children*. Washington, D.C.: Council for Exceptional Children, 1968.
   This monograph describes the materials and activities used in a preschool for disadvantaged children. The activities are organized under the titles of functions assessed by the ITPA. A remedial teacher will find practical activities for each of the ten areas assessed by the ITPA.

Dunn, L. M., and Smith, J. O. *The Peabody Language Development Kits, levels P, 1, 2, and 3*. Circle Pines, Minn.: American Guidance Service, 1966.
   This series consists of four kits, each for a different level of ability. Kit P is for three- and four-year-old children, kits 1, 2, and 3 for successively higher levels of ability, kit 3 being for children with about seven- and eight-year ability. Although designed primarily for classroom use, the activities can be used for smaller groups and for individual children. Many materials are included and the manual gives step-by-step directions for the teacher. Although many of the activities promote development in visual-motor areas (and even haptic abilities), the activities are weighted in the direction of auditory-vocal experiences.

Bush, W. J., and Giles, M. T. *Aids to psycholinguistic teaching*. Columbus, Ohio: Charles E. Merrill, 1969.
   This book describes materials and activities for each of the subtest functions of the ITPA. The activities are grouped according to the grade level for which they are appropriate, from first to sixth grade. For the remedial teacher who is looking for materials and procedures for ameliorating disabilities found on the ITPA, this book will furnish numerous suggestions.

Minskoff, E., Wiseman, D., and Minskoff, J. G. *The MWM program for language abilities*. In preparation.

This book, with associated instructional materials, includes detailed instructions to the remedial teacher on the development of ITPA functions. A task analysis of the functions has been made and remedial procedures for each are presented in a step-by-step program.

Rupert, H. A. 1971. *A sequentially compiled list of instructional materials for remediational use with the ITPA.* Washington, D.C.: Council for Exceptional Children.

This publication categorizes commercial instructional materials under each function of the ITPA. Remedial teachers will find ready reference to instructional materials for each of the disabilities revealed by ITPA assessment.

Computer-based resource units for special education. State University College at Buffalo, N.Y.

Appropriate activities are available for the various functions evaluated by the ITPA.

References

Amoss, H. 1936. *Ontario School Ability Examination.* Toronto: Ryerson Press.

Bateman, B. 1965. *The Illinois Test of Psycholinguistic Abilities in current research: Summaries of studies.* Urbana: University of Illinois Press.

———— 1963. *Reading and psycholinguistic processes of partially sighted children.* Council for Exceptional Children Monographs, Series A, No. 5.

Bateman, B., and Wetherell, J. 1965. Psycholinguistic aspects of mental retardation. *Mental Retardation,* April, 3 (2), 8–13.

Beery, K. E., and Buktenica, R. A. 1967. *The Beery-Buktenica Developmental Test of Visual Motor Integration.* Chicago: Follett Publishing Co.

Bender, L. 1962. *The Bender Visual Motor Gestalt Test for children.* Los Angeles: Western Psychological Services.

Bereiter, C., and Engelmann, S. 1966. *Teaching disadvantaged children in the preschool.* Englewood Cliffs, N.J.: Prentice-Hall.

Bilovsky, D., and Share, J. 1965. The ITPA and Down's syndrome: An exploratory study. *American Journal of Mental Deficiency,* 70 (1), 78–82.

Burgemeister, B., Blum, L. H., and Lorge, T. 1954. *Columbia Mental Maturity Scale.* New York: World Book.

Bush, W. J., and Giles, M. T. 1969. *Aids to psycholinguistic teaching.* Columbus, Ohio: Charles E. Merrill.

Chalfant, J., and Scheffelin, M. 1969. *Central processing disfunctions in children: A review of research.* Washington, D.C.: U.S. Government Printing Office.

Chall, J. 1967. *Learning to read: The great debate.* New York: McGraw-Hill.

189

Dillon, E. J. 1966. An investigation of basic psycholinguistic and reading abilities among the cerebral palsied. Doctoral dissertation, Temple University.

Dunn, L. M. 1965. *The Peabody Picture Vocabulary Tests.* Circle Pines, Minn.: American Guidance Service.

Dunn, L. M., and Smith, J. O. 1966. *The Peabody Language Kits.* Circle Pines, Minn.: American Guidance Service.

Fernald, G. 1943. *Remedial techniques in basic school subjects.* New York: McGraw-Hill.

Ferrier, E. E. 1966. An investigation of the ITPA performance of children with functional defects of articulation. *Exceptional Children,* May, 32 (9).

Foster, S. 1963. Language skills for children with persistent articulation disorders. Doctoral dissertation, Texas Women's University.

Frostig, M., and Horne, D. 1964. *The Frostig program for the development of visual perception: Teachers guide.* Chicago: Follett Publishing Co.

Frostig, M., Le Feuer, W., and Whittlesley, J. 1964. *Developmental Test of Visual Perception.* 2nd ed. rev. Palo Alto, Calif.: Consulting Psychologist Press.

Garber, M. 1968. Ethnicity and measures of educability. Doctoral dissertation, University of Southern California.

Getman, G. L., *et al.* 1968. *Developing learning readiness.* Manchester, Mo.: McGraw-Hill.

Goodenough, F. 1962. *Draw-a-Man Test.* In F. Goodenough, *The measurement of intelligence by drawings.* New York: World Book.

Goodenough, F., Maurer, K., and Van Wagenen, M. J. 1940. *Minnesota Preschool Scale.* Minneapolis: Educational Test Bureau.

Hamlin, C. S. 1962. A study using the Illinois Test of Psycholinguistic Abilities in the determination of the language abilities of hearing impaired children. Master's dissertation, University of Kansas.

Harris, D. B. 1963. *Children's drawings as measures of intellectual maturity.* New York: Harcourt, Brace, and World.

Hart, N. W. M. 1963. The differential diagnosis of the psycholinguistic abilities of the cerebral palsied child and effective remedial procedures. *Special Schools Bulletin* (Brisbane, Australia), August, 5 (2).

Hirsch, E. D. 1963. Training of visualizing ability by the kinesthetic method of teaching reading. Master's dissertation, University of Illinois.

Hirshoren, A. 1969. A comparison of the predictive validity of the revised Stanford-Binet Intelligence Scale and the Illinois Test of Psycholinguistic Abilities. *Exceptional Children,* March, 35 (7).

The Impact of Head Start. 1969. Vol. 1. Columbus, Ohio: Westinghouse Learning Corporation–Ohio University.

Johnson, D. J., and Myklebust, H. R. 1967. *Learning disabilities: Educational principles and practice.* New York: Grune and Stratton.

Karnes, M. B. 1969. *Research and development program on preschool disadvantaged children.* Washington, D.C.: Bureau of Research, U.S. Department of Health, Education and Welfare.

Karnes, M. B., *et al.* 1968. *Activities for developing psycholinguistic skills with preschool culturally disadvantaged children.* Washington, D.C.: Council for Exceptional Children.

Kass, C. E. 1966. Psycholinguistic disabilities of children with reading problems. *Exceptional Children,* April, 32 (8), 533–539.

Kephart, N. C. 1960. *The slow learner in the classroom.* Columbus, Ohio: Charles E. Merrill.

Kirk, S. A. 1968. Illinois Test of Psycholinguistic Abilities: Its origin and implications. In J. Hellmuth (ed.), *Learning disorders,* vol. 3. Seattle: Special Child Publications.

—— 1967. Amelioration of mental disabilities through psychodiagnostic and remedial procedures. In G. A. Jervis (ed.), *Mental retardation.* Springfield, Ill.: Charles C. Thomas.

—— 1966. *The diagnosis and remediation of psycholinguistic disabilities.* Urbana: University of Illinois Press.

—— 1962. *Educating exceptional children.* Boston: Houghton Mifflin.

—— 1958. *Early education of the mentally retarded—an experimental study.* Urbana: University of Illinois Press.

Kirk, S. A., and McCarthy, J. J. 1961. The Illinois Test of Psycholinguistic Abilities—an approach to differential diagnosis. *American Journal of Mental Deficiency,* November, 66 (3), 399–412.

Kirk, S. A., McCarthy, J. J., and Kirk, W. D. 1968. *The Illinois Test of Psycholinguistic Abilities.* Rev. ed. Urbana: University of Illinois Press.

Lombardi, T. P. 1970. Psycholinguistic abilities of Papago Indian children. *Exceptional Children,* March, 36 (7), 485–494.

Luria, A. R. 1963. *The mentally retarded child.* New York: Macmillan.

McCarthy, J. J. 1957. Qualitative and quantitative differences in the language abilities of young cerebral palsied. Doctoral dissertation, University of Illinois.

McCarthy, J. J., and Kirk, S. A. 1961. *The Illinois Test of Psycholinguistic Abilities.* Urbana: University of Illinois Press.

—— 1963. *The construction, standardization, and statistical characteristics of the Illinois Test of Psycholinguistic Abilities.* Urbana, Ill.: Institute for Research on Exceptional Children.

McCarthy, J. M. 1965. Patterns of psycholinguistic development of mongoloid and non-mongoloid severely retarded children. Doctoral dissertation, University of Illinois.

Macione, J. R. 1969. Psychological correlates of reading disability as defined by the Illinois Test of Psycholinguistic Abilities. Doctoral dissertation, University of South Dakota.

McLeod, J. 1965. Some psychological and psycholinguistic aspects of severe reading disability in children. Doctoral dissertation, University of Queensland, Australia.

Meyers, P. 1963. A comparison of language disabilities of young spastic and athetoid children. Doctoral dissertation, University of Texas.

Money, J., Alexander, D., and Walker, H. T., Jr. 1965. *A Standard Road Map Test of Direction Sense.* Baltimore: Johns Hopkins Press.

Monroe, M. 1932. *Children who cannot read.* Chicago: University of Chicago Press.

National Advisory Committee on Handicapped Children, U.S. Department of Health, Education and Welfare, Office of Education. 1968. *Special education for handicapped children: The first annual report of the national advisory committee on handicapped children.* Washington, D.C.: Department of Health, Education and Welfare.

Nielson, J. M. 1946. *Agnosia, apraxia, aphasia: Their value in cerebral localization.* 2nd ed. New York: Paul B. Hoeber.

Olson, J. L. 1961. Deaf and sensory aphasic children. *Exceptional Children,* April, 27 (7), 422–424.

——— 1960. A comparison of sensory aphasia, expressive aphasia and deaf children on the Illinois Test of Psycholinguistic Abilities. Doctoral dissertation, University of Illinois.

Osgood, C. E., and Sebeok, T. A. (eds.) 1965. *Psycholinguistics.* Bloomington: Indiana University Press.

Painter, G. 1966. The effect of a rhythmic and sensory motor activity program on perceptual motor spatial abilities of kindergarten children. *Exceptional Children,* October, 33 (2), 113–116.

Paraskevopoulos, J., and Kirk, S. A. 1969. *The development and psychometric characteristics of the revised Illinois Test of Psycholinguistic Abilities.* Urbana: University of Illinois Press.

Ragland, G. G. 1964. The performance of educable mentally handicapped students of differing reading ability on the ITPA. Doctoral dissertation, University of Virginia.

Raven, J. C. 1947. *Progressive Matrices.* New York: Psychological Corp.

Reichstein, J. 1963. Auditory threshold consistency: A basic characteristic for differential diagnosis of children with communication disorders. Doctoral dissertation, Columbia University.

Ryckman, D. B. 1966. The psychological processes of disadvantaged children. Doctoral dissertation, University of Illinois.

Sievers, D. J. 1955. Development and standardization of a test of psycholinguistic growth in preschool children. Doctoral dissertation, University of Illinois.

Sloane, H. L., and MacAulay, B. D. 1968. *Operant procedures in remedial speech and language training.* Boston: Houghton Mifflin.

Smith, J. O. 1962. *Effects of a group language development program upon the psycholinguistic abilities of educable mental retardates.* George Peabody College Special Education Monograph No. 1.

Sutton, P. R. 1963. The relationship of visualizing ability to reading. Master's dissertation, University of Illinois.

Terman, L. M., and Merrill, M. A. 1960. *Stanford-Binet Intelligence Scale: Combined L-M form.* New York: Psychological Corp.

Thurstone, L. L. 1938. *Primary mental abilities.* Psychometric Monographs. Chicago: University of Chicago Press.

——— 1940. *A factorial study of perception.* Psychometric Monographs. Chicago: University of Chicago Press.

Thurstone, L. L., and Thurstone, T. G. 1953. *SRA Primary Mental Abilities Test*. Chicago: Science Research Associates.

Thurstone, T. G. 1949. *Learning to think series*. Chicago: Science Research Associates.

Wechsler, D. 1949. *Wechsler Intelligence Scale for children*. New York: Psychological Corp.

Wepman, J. M. 1958. *Auditory Discrimination Test*. Chicago: published by the author.

Wiseman, D. E. 1965. The effects of an individualized remedial program on mentally retarded children with psycholinguistic disabilities. Doctoral dissertation, University of Illinois.

Index